The Ghost Forest

The Ghost Forest

new and selected poems

kimiko hahn

 **W. W. NORTON & COMPANY**
Independent Publishers Since 1923

For information about permission to reproduce selections from this book, write to
Permissions, W. W. Norton & Company, Inc., 500 Fifth Avenue, New York, NY 10110

For information about special discounts for bulk purchases, please contact
W. W. Norton Special Sales at specialsales@wwnorton.com or 800-233-4830

Manufacturing by Lakeside Book Company
Book design by Chris Welch
Production manager: Anna Oler

ISBN 978-1-324-08606-2

W. W. Norton & Company, Inc., 500 Fifth Avenue, New York, NY 10110
www.wwnorton.com

W. W. Norton & Company Ltd., 15 Carlisle Street, London W1D 3BS

10 9 8 7 6 5 4 3 2 1

for Ava and for Luca

my hearts

Contents

The Ghost Forest

Foreign Bodies (2020)

Brain Fever (2014)

Likeness (2017–18)

Toxic Flora (2010)

The Narrow Road to the Interior (2006)

The Artist's Daughter (2002)

Mosquito and Ant (1999)

Volatile (1999)

The Unbearable Heart (1995)

Earshot (1992)

Air Pocket (1989)

The Ghost Forest

A ghost forest is a real phenomenon: when sea levels rise, the waters flow farther inland. When salt water seeps into a freshwater marsh, the trees and vegetation rot then die off. The remains are a ghost forest of bleached-out trees. *Phantom limbs.*

A grove of memory. A marsh of forms. Listing shade. Conflicted shadows.

Erasures. Then again, an effort against erasure—*that ghosting.*

Of course, there are ghosts you don't see. Can't see or don't realize. Some you do not acknowledge. (I know, I know—*mother*, again.) Some you hear in the ethereal-sounding *g–h–o–s–t*.

Whatever happens with us, your body / will haunt mine—Adrienne Rich wrote in her unnumbered "Floating Poem."

A reservoir of letters.

These pieces go back in time so on the last page the earliest apparition comes to light.

A Riotous Disorder

She mistakes one word for another—
Something her brain naturally concocts.
Her unruly gray matter and her heart
Mistake one word for an other—
Razor for *river, cistern* for *sister*.
Even *cock* for *clock*.
She mistakes one word for a mother—
A safe her brain naturally unlocks.

The Calculation of Nothing

When it comes to counting and the honeybee,
who knew that the creature knew
nothing, that is, the very idea of none—
not a small thing when it comes to zero.
Only primates and one bird have passed the test
that even some civilizations could not picture.

The Inca, though, used a system of knots
to store their numbers: *aught* could be
as much a position as a hunger if a new crop,
let's say, amounted to none.
Honeybees get nothing, too, but
what does *knowing* mean? Past research

shows that as stars cycled past,
cosmologists and philosophers could not
agree on *nothing* (agreement to a bee matters little)
—that's nothing new—like ancient climate change
where no one survived unless
invited onto the ark in twos, though

some rascals should've been counted, too,
shouldn't have been passed over.
(I myself know the eight sailor knots.) I wish
I could just be counted like a bee
darting then resting in the dark for renewal.
Or like Siddhartha under a banyan,

I could sit until one with none. Anonymous
as an arithmetical creature, too.
Just sing and sip together as in eras past

—as when Incas fingered quipu knots. As when
an empty pistil meant a bee would
seek nectar blossoming anew:

the tiny workers knew when to quit
and when to flit. I know what's opinion
and what makes bee and woman. We two
have come to count on hives and buzz past
the knowledge of *not*. This world
is a knotty place for a being to enumerate. Yes,

a queen bee, second to none,
recalculates after scoring a new pasture—
not unlike my own zeroing in.

To be a daughter and to have a daughter

can forecast at-odds relationships
especially when the mother hazards to write
on her own *ours*, what time's left
while keeping the baby safe
from herself as she and the baby wail
one in the crib, the other on the floor to wail
with the vacuum cleaner so the daughter
can't hear mama-drowning, so the new relationship
isn't all arithmetic and geometry, all right
angles barely connecting. What is left
at dusk, still tender and safe,
you couldn't pluck and lock in a safe—
not unlike a girl calf and her mama whale,
two generations of breaching daughters
applauded by tourists on a ship
but, more likely, if they are right
whales, or what species are left
of those docile equatorial pods, never left
by men hunting their fat. They are not safe.
Larger than grays, smaller than blue whales,
the very buoyant mother and son or daughter
enjoy a year-long relationship
unless whalers spy these "right
whales to hunt." Funny, given the mariner's rite
to trick a man to think he'd been left
for the sharks without the safety

of pity or prayer—then that whaler would wail
for his own mother, wife, or daughter.
When it comes to daughter-mother relationships—

I've written on both till there's nothing left
without breaching safety, without whaling.
After all, I love daughters and I love ships.

The Ghost Forest

Neighbors call the stands of pine
a *ghost forest*—because when glaciers melt,
the sea steals onto the land, the salt
seeps in, and long-established marshes,

once fresh, now salt, seize
from bleach and blacken at the roots—
true, grubby shrubs, grasses, stands

of sweet-gum and loblolly pine
are less susceptible to the long-
visiting floods that now belong
to those insinuating sea waters. True,

the stranger sea and swindler salt water
are lodgers that coax their salt tenderly
into the tendrils that have rooted one

to home until one is rooted out.
True, the residents have lived long through
the come-ons—not just the flashes of seizure
nor a familiar's bolt—look—

after a drought, after the salt waters move in
without being seen, every thing
turns to a moldering spine so that now
anyone who remains in a cul de sac
longs to drive off—but on what route
when in the rear view, the dying stand

where once the homestead stood?
This afternoon, ruin takes root
at the threshold. Futures are salted away
in family cemeteries. Tell me
what belongs here more than
these morbid pine roots? How to see that

these roots can withstand the water from
long rains but not the sea? Spring tidings
are not from pine saplings but assault.

On *Viscera*

By chance, gazing out the window,
I notice a squall of white feathers
—maybe a pillow fight in the alley—
and rise for a real look
into the November gray to see
a hawk clutching a pigeon in its beak.
I jerk open the window
but the hawk just stares
into the wind-blown feathers
toward me in my bedroom
—not a really safe place either—
then takes off for better purchase
to devour the meat
in its claws and beak. Frozen
at this window, I notice
on my sill a feather—
a keepsake of the real,
proof of a pain that is real,
that mess of pigeon
on street or branch. I don't want
to think about beaks. Or
windows or feathers that recollect
an image of innards. Who
would want to reel at the sight
of one's own bowels,
brash red and bile?
What infernal beak can break
the brain's shuttered window to see
—a mother and father
on a pull-out feather bed,
the wall too shaking—

the entrails of the unconscious
as real as bark and branch, as great
as wings lifting, as sharp as a beak
with an atrocity called supper?
Through this outer-borough window

I am claws and beak and feathers.
I am blunt window. I am realizing
branch as a root shaking.

ERASING *HONOR*
for daughters

Her mother agreed to let them kill her

favored

a   brutal

feed

*

struck by an ax fifteen times

the woman ran away

the ax

received

a death

dealing

soul

*

because   she is an adulterer

        caught

                                                              on the

                blood clotted

        border

                        she
                                failed

                                                              the   border

*

After

                                        gently reinserting   and stitching her

                                unconscious

        anchored

light

treated her and cared for her for weeks

*

but for the
            light

she has no one; no mother has come, no father,

            no one to bring fresh

mountains and deserts   *and*

    a   borrowed

            night

*

Her mother agreed to let them kill

       the woman's   house

*

Her mother agreed to let them

   arrest
                 the woman's

                                         safe

*

I shivered when I saw

           the root

   impotent

large

vengeful

the woman is now
able to speak, but not   remember

*

swift, brutal

root

*

the story

shivered
and drove
the root

away

*

the story

                will erode

         the
morning   a distant relative   knocked on the couple's door

and was met by

              a   bed bleeding profusely

*

the story

              will   tend

                              unmarked graves

Found Lines for a Ghazal on Water

her family avoids any contact with the water.

Her youngest son has scabs on his arms, legs and chest where the bathwater

enforcement of water

strengthening water

untreated human waste has flowed into rivers and washed onto beaches.
   Drinking water

Jennifer knows not to drink the tap water

The liquid in those lagoons and shafts can flow through cracks in the earth
   into water

decade ago, awful smells began coming from local taps. The water

put their house on the market, but because of the water

reinvigorate the drinking water

cavities until the family stopped using tap water.

violated water

Found Lines for a Ghazal on *Nearly 1,000 Birds*

around 200 dead birds. Some days, no birds die. The nearly 1,000 dead birds

but the carpet of bird [carcasses]

how important it is for buildings to turn off their lights during bird

blown away" by how many birds

the temperature had been unusually high and the birds

When the temperatures dropped and the wind shifted, a huge number of birds

At the Field Museum, dead birds . . .

. . . turned over to a flesh-eating beetle colony that cleans the birds

Mr. Stotz said that the high concentration of dead birds

A handful of clippings. A basket of acrostics. A cupboard of conceits.

Playing with given forms, sometimes a sestina, say, works out as a sestina. Other times, the sestina becomes a rough draft. And yet the ghost of the sestina remains in the realized poem. And, of course, an erasure possesses its own redolence. Like a grandmother you met once. Or who your mother said you met when you were an infant. Or you never met at all.

There are other mothers and grandmothers. Some younger than yourself. Others born centuries before you.

The ghost of a ghazal.

A flask of quartinas.

Along the way, one ghost took shape from a pain so thorough nothing remained. Except mist.

Scent of salt. Taste of brine. A faint roar when I lie down on the futon

—*who are you talking to?*—

on a bed of apostrophes. A rough *raft*.

(When my mother died, my sister-in-law said, You will talk to her.)

The Earth's Day

Grain and water keep us alive.
Like plants, we drink the sunlight
Then ballad and lullaby.
With animals, we're coincident.

Plants sip up the sunlight.
The clouds sip from rivers.
With animals coincident,
The storms drink from streams.

When clouds sip from rivers,
The children drink their mama's milk.
The streams drink to storm.
The mamas drink from stars.

The children drink their mama's milk—
So light and tempest.
The mamas drink from stars.
The stars drink from where

There's light and tempest.
Just as grain and water keep alive,
The stars drink from where
A ballad lulls *bye-bye*.

On *Pleasing*

Like echoes in a seashell
held gingerly to the ear,
bright as a mother and baby's *please,*
early memory is a white sheet:

held gingerly for years
the baby laughs or sobs or sleeps.
Early memory is a white sheet
remembered as *peas* and *appease.*

The baby laughs or sobs or sleeps and
sounds separate from noise to events
remembered as *peas* and *appease.*
While she listens and hears

sounds separate from noise to events,
from blur to fidelity.
While the girl listens and hears
she recalls *peas* as *appease.*

Both blur and fidelity
echo in her seashell.
She recalls *peas* as *appease*
brighter than her mother and baby's pleas.

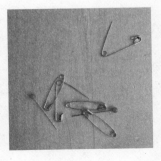

Not Nothing Again

I think of nothing but wind
or the black universe
though we see the sky bestrewn
with stars and planets.

Or see the black universe
as a chest of puzzles and toys
with stars and planets.
A circle with rings.

As if a chest of puzzling toys,
I wonder about my pink bear,
a circus with rings,
and a carousel of armadillos.

I wander with my pink bear.
I think of nothing as wind.
Also, as a carousel of armadillos
and bees strewn across the sky.

A Revelation with Two Lines from Yeats

Turning and turning in the widening gyre
The falcon cannot hear the falconer;
The cyclone cannot feel the air;

The drain disavows the water—
The roof's an outright liar.
Turning and turning in the widening gyre

The rancher cannot break her mare.
She's broke and both will soon retire—
The cyclone cannot hear the air.

The teacher's a screen, he'll soon retire
"What is theory, what is crossfire."
Turning and turning in the widening gyre

The children think they're scoring higher,
But they just spin the virtual where
The cyclone cannot see the air.

Who stays when oceans boil over?
Who returns when pavement catches fire?
Turning and turning in the widening gyre
The cyclone cannot flee the air.

The Toxicologist at Home

I literally lurch from thing to thing
with more curiosity than patience
to accost what cannot be seen.
Neither incensed nor senseless

I possess more curiosity than patience
unlike the crown-of-thorns sea star.
Not *not* incensed or senseless.
More, prickly. Or barbed.

Unlike the crown-of-thorns sea star
I do not possess deadly spikes.
I'm just prickly. Or barbed.
At times, metaphysically toxic.

Alas, I do not possess deadly spikes.
I do not turn myself inside out.
At times, metaphysically toxic
I belong to a crown-of-thorns sea star.

So I don't turn myself inside out
I lurch from thing to literal thing.
I long to be a crown-of-thorns sea star
to accost what cannot be seen.

Ode to "Not for these / the paper nautilus / constructs her thin glass shell."

I agree. Not for presidential reach or
an academic's tenure, no,

each is born fully formed
then readies for her young,

which is the point of life
and in this we abide and hope—

dear Mother, mother me,
so mercenaries never line, hook, or sink me.

ERASING THE *GHOST FOREST*

The   young
          predict
                                        intensified   spells and
the synergy of fire and salt

          just a few

               evoke graveyards

*

                                        sawgrass and black needle rush were

a clue   to   where

               Fires   travel on top of standing water

*

                                        If you're lucky, velvety tufts of cordgrass

               bark like alligator

          and crabs

*

Gedan has learned to read   forests

*

Gedan has learned to read

salt water

*

Gedan has learned to read

marsh

*

more intense   spells

conjure the

migrating

window into   the rest of the world

*

The menace

is a

fickle

ghost

27

Against Opulence

a glosa with Hardy's "The Convergence of the Twain"

Over the mirrors meant
   To glass the opulent
The sea-worm crawls—grotesque, slimed, dumb, indifferent.
Yes, in disaster's aftermath, *court*
is not *royal accommodation,*
more, the verb *to court,*
courting disaster on titanic liners
or inside houses built on stilts
along the salty coasts.
Over the mirrors meant
to reflect the complexion
of statesmen in staterooms
there are shadows of ghosts—
finned and gilled and with
scales that do not measure gold.
And currents cannot wait
To glass the opulent
because more than reflection
there's refraction. More than
strands of jewels, I see scrawls
—iambic lines drafted in silt,
verses ending in heroic couplet—
on the ocean floor, where after all
The sea-worm crawls—
Still, if I only see the abyssal zone
versus waves of plankton and sun,
volcanic episodes will be missed.
Islands of plastics will swirl,
mid-ocean, unnoticed.
In my compact, I too reflect
grotesque, slimed, dumb, indifferent.

Organized Decays
a glosa with Dickinson's #1010

Crumbling is not an instant's Act
A fundamental pause
Dilapidation's processes
Are organized Decays—

The hoarder's house is also home
to sad circulars, abject mites,
as well as beatific bird tracks.
The hoarder is father to daughters
and a trove of rubble:
mother's brush, paintbrush, plastic sacks.
Crumbling is not an instant's Act.

It's true, too, that *Ruin is formal—*
a dart or shadow
on the dining table gnaws
at candles and place mats.
Meantime, he aims to save—
what? a childhood noise?
A fundamental pause

with his weekend papa
who was at the plant
or with a new missus
(a floozy from a jazz joint)?
Turns out, Ruin is *Father*
when *fathering* excess.
Still, *Dilapidation's processes*

can be a son's blessing if
the decades of wreckage
answer boyhood entreaties.
I'm the daughter who won't hold fast.
I am casting the dead.
The hundred hotel ashtrays
Are organized Decays.

Convergence
an ars poetica

Iambic lines drafted in silt
are revised when glaciers melt
so verses ending in heroic couplet
are more epigram than sonnet.

Revised when glaciers melt,
continents submit to a warning.
The land is more epigram than sonnet
—no—more erasure than given form.

As continents admit the warming
the coasts ebb and go.
Erasure gives them form.
Plastic adds a climate of metaphor.

The coasts ebb and forgo
iambic lines drafted in silt.
Plastic adds a climax of metaphor—
ending in pyrrhic couplet.

Quarantine is never far. Certainly not far from the threshold when simple tasks grind down to questions. How to translate that—?

asagao ni / tsurube torarete / moraimizu
Kaga no Chiyo

the morning glory twines around the bucket rope—i'll go to my neighbor for water

the morning glory twists around the bucket rope so look for water elsewhere

asagao twists around the well ladle so look for water elsewhere

the morning glory twines around the bucket rope—i'll see my neighbor for water

a morning glory around the well ladle—ask next door for water

We stocked up on paper products, canned peaches, and rice. The morning glories translated themselves. And I wondered if aloneness constitutes an eighth kind of Ambiguity.

Even so, when we each came down with a fever, one neighbor placed homemade soup on our step. Another, a sack of fruit. Plumbs. I mean—plums.

Villanelle with a Line Borrowed from Bishop

The child looks out the window at the peeling barn.
The mother sits on the roof and waves at her.
The grandmother sings to the marvelous stove.

The child has put away her own Marvel Stove
because her grandmother is baking real bread.
The child looks out the window at the peeling barn.

The two inside are preparing dinner for three.
(If the mother comes down from the roof.)
The grandmother sings to the marvelous stove

a song about some mother on some roof
(likely the mother that is her daughter).
The child looks out the window at the peeling barn.

The child hums along while she stands
to survey her reeling barn and to hear as
The grandmother sings to the marvelous stove.

She's drawn at least half a dozen barns today.
She stops humming and sings her own song.
She looks at her mother atop the peeling barn while
the grandmother sings to *marvel* the stove.

In Our Living Room

a glosa with Bishop's "In the Waiting Room"

The waiting room was bright
and too hot. It was sliding
beneath a big black wave,
another, and another.

At home, Mother was always with
the baby in another room. Tonight
under the windows' dark winter,
we two were sitting alone
on the couch, spot lit in a circle
from an overhead lamp. Here
another, and another

of her words sounded like
Paia Auntie's black beach
or clammy cave.
I looked at Mother's red lips.
This time her words were not
bidding "try behave":
beneath a big black wave,

she kept talking about blood
until little black dots
floated around like dust blinding
my eight-year-old face.
"And, out of the blue, blood
will soak your panties." I was sliding
and too hot. It was sliding,

the room. I didn't want blood
without wound or warning.
But there was no flight
from the waves of her voice
in the room of that room.
For once, I hoped she wasn't right.
The waiting room was bright.

if is a conjunction
with lucille clifton

if there is a river
more beautiful than this
bright as the blood
red edge of the moon   *if*
i can conjure such
radiance and safety
as expressed shelter
then my task as woman
will be quenched.

yes, moon, yes, calendar
if there is a river
that will cleanse
my generous
innermost abyss,
then echo syllables
of consonance.
after all, red is a wish,

more beautiful than this
—this river that men call foul
and view a girl infirm
though they brood
if she does not breed.
yes, a woman pronounces

her throbbing inside
bright as the blood,
reliable as the planets.
kind as the cocoon.

crafty as a paper.
i know girls who've gone
mad. some left us livid.
we owe them, to commune
with the *red edge of the moon*   *if*

ABRACADABRA

Art Is All, the family motto, was

Bidden in a childhood tucked

Right against a gloomy wood.

All we girls could do to keep spirits

Contained—to keep ourselves

Alive as the Art that was,

Dare I say, really *Father*—

Almost annihilated us daughters.

Brave little shamanesses, we

Reveled in contradiction with

Artful spells, shrewd bailiwick.

Contrapuntal Opening with a Line from Millay

She is neither pink nor pale

She is neither grain nor bud

She is neither beach nor sand

She is neither pillow nor feather

She is neither nipple nor bottle

She is neither out nor outside
nor put out nor outstanding

Not jump rope or jacks (not even
parcheesi)

—not side or siding—

—not mica or formica—

She is neither black nor gray nor
cirrus

She is not Japanese or *Japanese*

She is neither stratus nor cumulous   Not single Not binary Not theoretical

Yes—dialectical—yes

After Sonnet #12

When ice slats glut the salty flow by the shore's chance dogwood; when those same branches offer buds but clench again in sudden snap; when a sultry sun melts such stiffness until the season turns to arctic stream—arctic, tropic, arctic, tropic—and the earth's autumnal tilting, then I'll see how infallibly we creak, falter, fall, and admit the brusque in brisk weather that weathers also spirit— Even so, we'll bring home a branch to force a last bloom atop our shaky nightstand.

In my vanity I keep a stash of hotel shower caps and cotton swabs. Along with safety pins.

It's possible that I'll find mother there, among sewing items in a blue cookie tin. Three needles. Spool of black thread. Crane-shaped scissors. U-shaped scissors. Bonefolder. A doll's canvas shoe.

A tin of notions.

A wooden cigar box of canceled stamps.

A corpse—I mean *copse* of consonance.

Seeing to Etiquette

The crabgrass and dandelions on the unmown lawn
attract flocks of blackbirds and grackles and

they look like a neighborhood party,
walking in a line, arms-width apart, seeking evidence

except, of course, they're not overturning tufts of grass
for a shred of cloth or cigarette butt. I like the grass unmown.

I like that hopping about for no-see-ums. And now
the flocks lift off, again not unlike neighbors done

looking for a lost girl. *Lost*, as in, *we've lost her*.
As in, *she's dead*—though we dare not say the word, *dead*.

Herschel said it's one of the few taboos left in America, death.
To talk about it. And I see that. But today Nicole commented on

a bereavement note to Esther—maybe by way of reminding
that that's how things are seen to. Yes, they—the birds, that is—

take off in a single pall over the grove:
I hear their squawks and see the elms shaking.

Shuddering like neighbors. I like proprieties. And next,
I write a condolence to Nicole's father Peter. I like black birds.

Ode to *Love*

you

noted with excitement that the male was missing   the posterior part of its body

*It may be that all individuals pass through a stage in which they are males and
    then*
                    they're females

the head will soon be delivered to

you

Aubade: Feverish Speculation

Love
             might still be

a carcass in deep freeze until   someone   can clean and mount the skeleton

*
Love
                might still be

ice in a ditch

*
Love

can jettison   bodies   much the way lizards can shed their tails

*
                If something about tectonic movement is killing
Love
We wanted the kids to see

tissue samples, skin samples and eyeball samples

Ars Poetica

designed to see in the low light of the deep ocean

the   eye   is unusually large

Love
might still be under water
not spotted

A Student Suggests All the Women in Class Imagine Male Sexuality

unpredictable
            hard

            long and eel-like in appearance, can grow to stupendous lengths—
though ancient rumors of 55-foot specimens are probably exaggerated

a handful of
Love

a variety of parasite

    male

            excitement

Elegy

           Milton   *said*

                                                      left with

the
remains

            You can only   *Love*
      an ichthyologist

Ekphrasis

    quite near the surface, suspended vertically with   *head up, just*
        passively floating

and   *known as ryugu no tsukai, or "messenger from the sea god's palace."*

picture   *it*

Seeing Someone Seeing

A little girl with a cellphone camera
noticed a whale in the Buttermilk Channel
and clicked a shot of its aura,
just a random child with a camera.
How often do we see phenomena—
a robin or turtle hatching? or an angel
of a child with a camera
capturing her whale in the Buttermilk Channel?

Decades ago, I thought—*I've taken years to imagine an Asian American aesthetic. Of course, it's a complicated raft of many elements and for me, a reflection of Asian form, an engagement with content that may have roots in historical identity, together with a problematic—even psychological— relationship to language. One that spreads out beyond the personal.*

I know, I know—everyone has a psychological relationship to language. But this is a particular kind of anxiety. Some have said *melancholic*.

Affect. Effect.

Melancholic? A chest of children's books in *hiragana, kanji* flash cards, *karuta*. A picnic hamper of haiku.

Michael, my first poetry instructor, suggested we talk back to a poem. I absorbed that prompt into what would become my poetics. I have whole sequences that quarrel with *The Tale of Genji* or the translators. Really—how can one trust a translator—

How to trust *ghosts*?

And aren't allusions also ghosts? I know very well how the *Genji* characters alluded to writers from the past: in Genji's grief, Kanzuke Mineo's waka from the *Konkinshu* came to his thoughts. For me, a footnote must suffice—

> If you have hearts, cherries of Fukakusa—for this once, blossom in black.

Word of a friend's death brings this poem to mind. I trust the allusion. I depend on it.

I depend on the lines. As one might a red wheelbarrow.

A wheelbarrow of allusions.

(His *In a White Light* had not yet appeared.)

[Blossoming purple]
after Richard Wright

To think of a girl as **blossoming**
is to consider a **purple**
spiraling upward. **A**
bud **forgotten**
(even an **artichoke**!)
to safekeep. **In**
time the girl becomes **a**
perennial opening in the **dark**
of the mind's **cupboard**.

[Follow wherever]

after Richard Wright

In bedtime stories, a girl or girls must **follow**
instructions (or the wind) **wherever**
the concrete, the visible or **the**
voice (like that of a **tree**)
leads her. She walks a path until it **branches**,
then halts, fancies she'll **make**
a choice because choice isn't foretold. She **arches**
her back then her eyebrows. She finds herself **in**
a clearing where animals badger. **The**
possum says, *Light can be **torrid.***
*The moonlight more than the **sun**.*

[The whale already]

after Yosa Buson

What is endangered, **the**
rest of us ignore. The **whale**,
adored by children and cartoonists, **already**
dwindles. Even bycatch has **taken**
them. The tiny creatures they consume haven't **got**
a chance to outlast the warming. **A way**
to safeguard whales is deny ourselves **the**
car and its exhaust. The **moon**
sees us—at any cost—**alone**.

[The women first]

after Kobayashi Issa

She feared the undertow and **the**
sharks there where **women**
in her family collected seaweed, **first**
pulling up skirts, then taking a **turn**
at the best swaths of shore. *That's a **hazy***
recollection, Mother had said **over**
breakfast. *Also Grandma's kitchen,* **the**
*shadows smelling like a **tidal***
*current. I even feared the **flats.***

[Splash-splashing a]
after Takayanagi

The dog and baby are **splash-splashing**
so the ripples halo in **a**
kitchen puddle where another **child**
pours another pot of water on the tiles then **walks**
through while intoning **in**
a divine dialect she's conjured **for**
this sublime opportunistic **river**.

[In the garden]
after Uejima Onitsura

Every year flora and fauna **in**
all recesses fall extinct or **the**
species can only be seen in **garden**
or terrarium. Somewhere where **blooming**
is all hot house **white**
with mist and where laborers **are**
encouraging riotous **camellias**.

[Onion]
after Tada Chimako

Fragrance of **onion**
fills the building corridor as I **peel**
away from the apartment, **away**
from cable news, ***Seven***
Kinds of Ambiguity, vegetable **skins**
and melon rinds in the sink **and**
the blender left unwashed. **Nothing's**
to be done since Mother **left**.

[a wind blows in]
after Yûgen

Aging synapses lose tenacity and **a**
pulse dwindles to a vague **wind.**
Memory **blows**
—images are blown—**in**
this dusk. Yes, a **haze**
befalls my skull where even **this**
full moon misses the **evening**.

[I am paying]
after Richard Wright

I am searching for sublet signs, **I am**
circling classified ads. **Paying**
for another rebound, **rent**
will be my reward for leaving—**for**
my own peeling walls, for **the**
infested linoleum, the **lice**
on sheets, in sweaters, **in**
my hair. Here, how can **my**
chambers—the muscled one, the **cold**
one—unfreeze? Here in our **room**
I looked for keepsakes. **And**
a reason to stay put. **The**
dog? No. Maybe, the **moonlight**
across the dog. And the man's back, **too.**

The footnoted poems in *Genji* give rise to further thought—if allusions are ghosts, perhaps the quotes are a way to keep the person vivid.

> I wonder in jest if I could do without you.
> I gave it a try, to which I proved unequal.
>
> —Anonymous, *Kokin Wakashû*, 1025

That prompt from undergraduate days—to correspond with past poems, to talk back—was such a gift.

[Inside my body] i.
after Tada Chimako

Though unseeable we assume the **inside**—
tissue, blood, and bone appear in **my**
mind. The piss and shit before the **body**
evacuates. But also lodged is one's **death**,
in some form, unless expiring **is**
unforeseen like my mother's, **a**
crashing metal against metal. Her **soft**
self crushed on that **wintry**
parkway. Did the paramedic notice her **wart**?

[Inside my body] ii.
after Tada Chimako

On my stomach, I slip **inside**
the snow fort packed as **my**
hideaway. On my back, my **body**
is one with the ice. **Death**
is never near, I think I thought—**is**
death near a seven-year-old's **soft**
reluctance to leave the **wintry**
pleasure of worrying a **wart**?

[Inside my body] iii.
after Tada

The ceiling **inside**
the marriage where I rest **my**
comforter for his **body**
and mine, where we sleep beside **death**
like everyone else, **is**
as common as **a**
roof. The quiet is **soft**.
The air, a **wintry**
color of **wart**.

[Inside my body] iv.
after Tada

I don't know what's **inside**
a snoring head. **My**
sixty-year-old **body**
does know **death**
as the last reticence there **is**
because first Mother then Father became **a**
breath of **wintry**
weather. Common as a **wart**.

Ode to the Mud in Corona Park

Walk so silently that the bottoms of your feet become ears.

—Pauline Oliveros

After all, you persist this late winter
to offer history and souvenir
so I walk—as a teacher instructed—
listening to you with my feet. I hear
the slow creak of a glacier, ice sheets
breaking stone into terminal moraine.
I hear the waters in a glacial lake and rivulets.
Torrents turning earth to marsh.
Then, the Lenape hunted then the Dutch
used tufts and twigs for grazing animals.
I hear their lowing. I hear muskets.
I hear the metal on road and rail.
And after the rich enjoyed a quiet green resort,
there came dumping. Can you hear the tons
of ash? Can you hear the stench and infestation?
Can you hear the fur trappers and squatters?
I hear them and the locals collecting firewood.
I hear the lawns unrolled for the fair.
The vigils and games! (The crimes—
we can't forget the crimes—)
Hear the picnic benches and picnickers.
Hear the macadam. The gravel. Hear
new stampedes. New trains of thought.
New embraces. New ardor.
The centuries whisper to my feet.

Anaphora Using the Wilfred Owen Line "If you could hear, at every jolt"

If you could hear, at every jolt, the building quiver—

If you could hear fossils stirring—

If you could hear sand from the fathoms rise—

If you could hear calf thrum to whale—

If you could hear dogs pause still as a deer before bounding—

If you could hear bounding—

If you could hear a neighbor shout to her daughter—*stand in the door*—

If you could stand—

If you could hear what's not a fault—and is a fault—

You'd hear the earth sounding war—

Climate-Change Driven Winds Across Nonnative Grasslands Leave Maui Vulnerable on August 10, 2023

a golden shovel after Uejima Onitsura

even on the beach there's **no**
patch to **place**
belongings, **to**
rest on a **throw,**
but I stay **out**
of waves more scalding than any **bathwater,**
stay by the roar of flames that **sound**
like the cry **of**
a trillion **insects**

Ode to "When lilacs last in the dooryard bloom'd"

I cannot consider scent without you, I cannot
think that color so gay, so vernal, so Japanese
without you; not assassination nor any death in any spring. I think of you
and I am man-and-woman, flawed as a Lincoln,
welcoming as a window box, and so tenderly alliterative as to draw one near—
at times, perhaps, to withdraw from all—yes,
without you I am without pulse in that dooryard,

so, tell me finally, is *last* as in *the last time* or *to make something last*
—to hold, to hold you, to memorize fast—

Foreign Bodies

(2020)

During sophomore year *Hard Freight* came out and every-
one in Charles's workshop pored over his lines. The stanzaic
structures brought home what I'd learned growing up around
artists, growing up to intuit motifs and forms. His lines
reminded me of musical notation. *Divides. Rests. Repeats.*

Decades later, when looking for an epigraph, I thought of his
work and found—

Some things move in and dig down
                              whether you want them to or not.
          Like pieces of small glass your body subsumes when
                you are young . . .

I always pictured his photo on the cover but now I see that
there's a train. A train of his mind. Then realize the collection
published that year was *Bloodlines*. And flipping through, I
realized again how familiar the stanzaic patterns felt. Even
familial.

Signature. Breath mark. Ghost note.

Since childhood I look at things, like the side of a tenement
and mostly notice the pattern of windows, regular or offbeat.
It is the irregular that delights. Father taught us girls to see
in such a way. Mother taught us to trust what we cannot see.

Caesura.

Charms from *Foreign Bodies*

Nip in the Bud

Pull out a Queen Anne's Lace
By every gnarled tendril
To hone your skill at tatting
As well as thwart a rival

Reprisal

If a sweetheart aims to stray
For a neighbor's tryst
Secure a means to shake
Nettles on her sheets

Empathy

When you spy a horseshoe crab
Flipped over on the shore
Right it gently in the tide
And with your kin—a true rapport

Object Lessons

From Chevalier Quixote Jackson

What might happen to the collection if we let narrative and desire back in?
—Mary Cappello

To answer a wish to possess:
tuck a chess piece into a cheek.
To meet a hunger not to share:
swallow a kewpie doll whole.
To recall the rubber of a nipple:
suck on a pencil eraser.
Safekeep sincere assemblage

by stowing in a ribcage. Yes,
                              now I lay my
two pressed pennies
down to constant tissue.
*
Like Dr. Chevalier Quixote Jackson,
nineteenth-century laryngologist who

removed from tiny upper bodies
an involved collection of objects

—nails and bolts, radiator key,
a child's perfect attendance pin,

a Carry-Me-For-Luck medallion—

to lay into trays of cotton, yes,
like him, each child had hoarded some thing

inside her inmost chest.

*

Yes, because children crawl on the treacherous floor,
Chevalier, if I may,
                        removed then preserved every last one
along with stunning x-rays of needles

lodged in a small patient's lung. Also
a charm in the shape of a hound. Maybe

the hound who rescued him in childhood.
Maybe a jar of charms that won't leave go one's origin.

(Maybe *my* pooch who calms my errant heartbeats down.)
*

Origins: crime or act of preservation:
Saturn devoured his children

to save his own skin from divine betrayal.
Snow White's stepmother devoured

the girl's lung and liver—or so she believed.

My youngest, after Mother died, figured,
Grandma now lives inside my tummy

with dog and bird and fishy.
*

According to one biographer: *at one point other children blindfolded Jackson
and threw him into a coal pit, and he was rescued only after some mutt hap-
pened to find him unconscious.*
*

In my cigar box, a swallow

                    nest of pine

lined with feathers, bits of birch bark, and trash

for comfort can coincide with comforting;

from the shred of blankie inside her purse to

his rabbit-foot keychain

to the hair she plucks and swallows

in a cycle of self-harm called *Rapunzel.*

Chevalier archived them in shallow drawers

according to their kind.

*

The two girls could not unlock the door to their father's home. The girls could not open a window for the medical books leaning against the panes. The girls could neither pry open the bathroom window painted shut nor the cellar door where the carton of bleach and cans of stew were stacked against it. They could not find a ladder to climb to the bedroom window and check on a mahogany bedroom set—this, they knew to be surrounded by trash bags of mother's clothing that they'd tagged years ago for the Salvation Army. And, hopefully, on the nightstand, there was still a collection of ivory netsuke.

Also, a reclining ivory nude, female, used by nineteenth-century doctors.

The girls wondered what he made of that woman.

*

The doctor's x-rays captured
miniature binoculars, silver horse-charm, four open safety pins

lodged between tiny ribs.
Each feels like a story's climax

when the heroine, dropping into a cave,
discovers a treasure at bottom

that cannot be removed unless she answers these three questions:

What is the opposite of "cleave"?
Who savors rampion?
Why not rock an empty chair?
*

How to extract an open safety pin without scarring?
How to save the object without anesthesia?
How to preserve all two thousand foreign bodies?
*

A child crawls on the treacherous floor
appraising every object inside her mouth.

*

Dr. Jackson's work produced the modern endoscope for the upper airways
with the use of hollow tubes and illumination. To see inside. As if he could
see the image of the horse-beating that had *taken residence inside him like a
primal scene, told him where his body began and ended* . . .

*

        In the Emergency Room, surgeons also remove sex-related objects
                from the rectum (the ubiquitous light bulb or hamster)

                and from the perineum (straight pins and nails)
                and from the penis (rose stem with thorns).

        There's also the stripper flashing a razor in and out of her labia.

                      Alas, my imagination pales—

*

Newly coined terms—
Amylophagia, ingesting laundry starch
Cautopyreiophagia, ingesting burnt matches
Geomelophagia, raw potatoes
—all exemplifying specialized terms

within *Pica*, a disorder named after the Eurasian magpie *pica pica*,
known for its *morbid craving*.

(What does one turn to
when laundry starch, say, becomes no more—?)

*

Flashlight, trombone cleaner, curling iron, screw, battery: all up the bum!

*

In the local Savings & Trust I descend to the corridor below street level. A woman sits in a cool gray light updating client info, filing her nails, text messaging. I step up to the bulletproof window, slip my I.D. into the slot, smile, and wait. She looks from my photo to my face. "Which one?" she asks. "The smaller one," I reply. I am not able to say my ex-husband's name in this ceremony of twenty years. "Yes," she replies. And as she takes her key and mine, I think about this box as *incomplete transaction*: old wedding bands, diamond earrings twice worn, and Mother's jewelry—inherited and rarely worn. No— never worn. Safely kept. From myself.

Then there are bonds for the children. (I haven't ever checked the other one containing the deed with the new husband.)

*

What is down the hatch?
(A penny-sized harmonica, a pea-sized magnet, button batteries, jacks!)

What then is the fourth question?
(*What does that mean,* safe?)

To whom does the extracted foreign body belong?
(If you tuck a crucifix under your tongue, then Mama cannot hunt it down.)

Too hard to swallow? Or *swallow hard?*
(Nicole's missing charms: sewing machine, thimble, *Mother*)

*

The why:
playing around wicker chair
playing with a tin cup containing a white pearl button
alone on floor with lucky-shell bracelet
put toy in his mouth to hide from sister
child alone in room found hairpin under pillow
bored or unhappy
*

Dr. Jackson's Aphorisms:
Let your left hand know what your right hand does and how to do it.
Let your mistakes worry you enough to prevent repetition.
Nature helps, but she is no more interested in the survival of your patient
        than in the survival of the attacking pathogenic bacteria.
*

Yes, how to extract a barrette without further scarring?
How to store the object of your ardor, even to stay what harms
(junk drawer, purse, . . . flash drive)?

Yes, how to *persevere*
long enough to sound an alarm? to be alarming?
*

Somewhere I have a palm-sized clock,
green with a daffy cartoon face
that Daddy bought for me at the hospital
when we visited Mother who'd just had a baby.
And could that toy

be tucked away with puka shells, miniature sleigh, and
—and really, has the point of *an object lesson* come down to this—
Mother's plastic collar *stay*?

Objecting

Snap a photo on your phone
of items to ingest
never mind its clarity
the object is not the object

The Nest in Winter

In the father's shadowy hoard
pillows belch feathers across
mattress and floors:
what was an oriental rug, now
a carpet of scat, gone-astray socks,
calendars from rescue shelters
angling for checks.
There's nothing to toss
among the vivid tethers to
Mother. Maybe my mother, maybe father's.
There's no margarine container
any less pathetic than
a netsuke from Kyoto;
no expired sardine tin any less urgent
than a dozen aerograms; no
receipt less intimate
than their honeymoon photo
snapped in the local aquarium.
The adult daughter takes in
the spew,
pabulum that a bird feeds its nestling.

Grandpa-stays
Grandpa stays

The Ashes

I wake to the radiator gurgling
and the puppy snarfling to be let out.
Then feet crunch the reticent snow.
Before I was born, Mother sewed her own suits.
What do her ashes know?
*

Father shoved snow off the supine roof.
Mother crafted Christmas ornaments:
glue and glitter and red balls.
No tinsel, no angels.
Her death started in the living room.
*

For bonsai, pliers the size of a nail clipper,
spools of wire, and a fist-sized rock.
One bore a petite pomegranate,
never to eat, not to touch.
Her death began with a baseball bat.
*

In the vineyard, he secured the strongest cane
from training stake to fruiting wire.
Pruning with handsaw and lopper.
He'd leave a spur for the next season.
He shoved her away with direct objects.
*

In a cold snap if one pipe freezes,
the rest may freeze as well.
Even before the puppy stirs.
Even before a baby sister arrived
in Mother's arms in the misleading car.
*

After the war, after she met Father,
she smoked menthols but didn't cha-cha anymore.
She'd light up and blow smoke
out the apoplectic window.
He found the ashes on the sill.

*

Fireflies winked for mates or prey
outside the savvy window of my own first home
where I sewed a dress too smart to wear.
On the stereo, a bluesman cried,
I need my ashes hauled!

*

I tucked away our baby's pink layette
in circumspect mothballs
for a christening that never took place.
As well, a doll that Auntie crocheted.
More than anything, I love tidal pools.

*

I know her ashes are at Father's,
lost in his charnel of junk mail.
He claims that thieves have stolen the box,
his knob cutter and root hook.
He says *ashes aren't remains anyways.*

*

Winter stripped everything to limb
and dejected nest. No angels, no crèche.
I don't know whose recollections are suspect:
after leaving Maui, Mother learned to swim.
(She loved tidal pools more than anything.)

*

In my kitchen, logs blink in the fire—
through blinds, the wind blusters and
browbeaten trees creak in the orchard.
The rain pours then stops for sun. If
he lost Mother's ashes what more could I stand?
*

Omusubi tastes best on black beaches.
Because Mother never learned to swim,
she watched her five brothers from a blanket.
On the intransigent subway, I can't recall if I've passed
my station. Metal smells of being fertile again.
(His mother said *her social station—*)
*

Mother showed our little girl how to sift flour
and how to crank an eggbeater.
After Father lost her,
he barred us from his rooms and yard
where at night, long red worms
slithered up from the ground.
*

Mother's ashes know: before the puppy snarfles,
Father shoves snow off the supine roof;
for bonsai, use pliers the size of a nail clipper;
in the vineyard, the strongest canes;
in a cold snap, a hair dryer on frozen pipes;
fireflies winked for mates or prey outside
while I tucked away my baby's pink layette.
Mother's ashes know their box is in the living room
where she didn't cha-cha anymore.
But has winter stripped everything to nest?
In my kitchen, the logs blink in the fire and I know
omusubi tastes best on a *back* shore. I know, too,
she doggedly showed granddaughters how to graft flowers.

In graduate school, while most scholars were taken by theory, I was studying Japanese language and literature, a field that seemed barely touched by such heady stuff. Fortunately, one professor offered a graduate class designed to familiarize us with Barthes, Jameson, Cixous, et al. The theory that impressed me most then—and that has influenced me ever since—was Barbara Herrnstein Smith's *Poetic Closure*. In short: "the conclusion of a poem has a special status in the process, for it is only at that point that the total pattern—the structural principles which we have been testing—is revealed."

Melvin Dixon asked, "When is closure an ending?" Which led me to wonder the opposite.

(Did Sekou suggest—down an alley of dissonance? Did Meena add—in a bowl of iambs?)

A Dusting

However Mother has reappeared
—say, as motes on a feather duster—
scientists say the galaxy
was thus created. This daybreak
she seeds a cumulous cloud.

*

Wherever Mother is bound
she's joined *ashes ashes*
or dirt underfoot or bits
off Tower North and Tower South.
Repurpose does not arrive whole cloth.

*

From stardust, dust bunnies,
Dust Bowl, *Dust unto Dust,*

to Rukeyser's *silica*, Whitman's *boot-soles*,
and Dunbar's *What of his loving, what of his lust?*

to samples that astronomers collect—
dust is where the sparrow bathes herself.

*

"Not a cloud in the sky,"
Mother says as she hangs the laundry outside,
Father paints *en plein air*,
and we girls sweep crumbs under the rug.
This summer, Father sees
Inferno everywhere.

*

No dustups from little girls!
As a consequence, one scribbled
on the dustbins of history
and the other dusted
for fingerprints. And the mother?
The mother lived in a vacuum.

*

Inside the senseless corridors
the daughter cannot respire.
Inside the vulgar cosmic
the mother cannot be revived
in streaming wet traffic.

*

Nowadays, I lie down in the sunlight
to see my mama
moting around as sympathetic ash.
Yes, one morning whether misty or yellow
I'll be soot with her—

elegiac and original.

A Little Safe

In a toy safe, I locked
seven glass giraffes from Grandma
once displayed on her credenza.
After she lost her riddled lung,

the hospital lost all her remains.
Or so the story goes.
*

I treasure her charm,
a tiny box housing a dollar—
not that that would get me far in a pinch.
And, speaking of pinches, she said:

Don't let a boy into your purse.
But what does a mother rehearse?
*

On Wednesdays, half the fifth grade
left for Catechism Class, each

learning to save other souls
as if the chest, a cathedral. When

a cousin stepped out on his wife,
I called his other woman *a buttress*
and added, *You'd best send her flying.*
*

What I locked in my school locker
besides pop quizzes marked *C*,
a velvet coat, and *Tiger Beat*s:

a locket. From no one.
Like evidence in the cold case file
of thirteen hacked-up call girls.
*
If I could visit Antarctica
I'd visit a penguin papa on his long-winded stint
warming an egg on his feet. Still,

a girl should not show *le pied* ever
when around her father.
*
Yes, even in unkind terrain
the girl felt okay on a trek with a coyote

until they reached the apathetic border
and her heart broke from
its eight years of beating. The same
for the boy in the trunk. For

the hundreds of babies in tents.
I found that the stories are the faithful ones.
*
After Grandma lost her riddled lung,
the raccoon ransacked emergency
boxes of powdered milk in the pantry.

Cold cases of Squirt remained safe.
And the word, *safety*? Think rubbers. Think patrol.
Think *Glock*. Then think accidental discharge.
*

I found that in the Isua supracrustal belt,

flora had been frozen for billions of years,
secure until discovery. Throughout his home
Father entrusted his critical papers

to those catacombs of no recollection.

Alloy

An Apostrophe for Isamu Noguchi

Is stone the opposite of dust? And if so, are we then stone before dust? And
before that, some kind of betwixt? The mush inside a translucent chrysalis
turning cellophane-clear when, of a sudden, you can see the Monarch
throbbing and scratching its way into air—

unlike a centipede that lays eggs and curls around them with her hundred
  feet.
You said that *living in Japan our house was filled with centipedes.*
I became rather fond of them. I lost my fear. You know, when you kill one,
the two halves just walk off. Surely, they played in your mind all the way to
  your piece
"Even the Centipede,"

molded from Ibaraki clay—though you felt *in a medium like clay*
anything can be done; and stated, *I think that's dangerous. It's too fluid. Too*
  facile.
Under your instruction, I'll find what is too fluid for me and turn my
  scratching
away from facile to fossil

using hammer, chisel, and drill if lucky enough to come across the right quarry
and ask nice enough or pay enough for a crew to blast out the marble—
unless the material is residue from something else. *Glacial pain?*
I mean, *glacial moraine*

from my home on the Sound where a glacier once terminated then abandoned
  her boulders. I pick up a rock, rounded and chipped in the surf, then, back
    home,
like those who set Jizo on boulevard altars in Kyoto,
I tie a bib around its belly. I place it on our mantel. Like those women,
I, too, remember my baby unborn from betwixt

and *Japanese*. Japanese like those where dust storms blew farm families
to smithereens, then, blew desert through rows of barracks
surrounded by barbed wire. Even orphan babies with one drop of *Jap blood*
were seized from whatever charity for bowls of dust. And you,
Noguchi-sensei, volunteered yourself

into this incarceration limbo. You requested permission to build
a baseball diamond, swimming pool, and cemetery.
You entered Poston Internment where you knew yourself a Nisei,
that is, without the rights of a citizen: *request*, of course, *denied*.
(Not for nothing, you were despised on both sides.)
And as for centipedes

I'm not so much afraid as squeamish, which is different, and I've never
    killed one
by cutting it in half so I don't know about the two live sides. The split selves
not seeing eye-to-eye, I only know too well. You and I know
differently from parents

who realized alloy only from without, whereas the *coywolf*, say,
realizes coyote and wolf even if the composite isn't brought to light—
which leads me to wonder, maybe light is the opposite of stone,
say, lightning that cracks inside a cloud?

or coral that glows below the surface of the sea? or the full moon
that illuminates the shoji of the falling-asleep boy? I love
the firefly's serenading signals, patterned according to kind. *Kind*—
borders your parents and mine did not essentially heed. Yes, in my mind,
stone, water, light, etcetera

all come down to dust on a moth's wing, dust that's evolved
to keep her patterns cued for a mate and to keep her blanketed in the
    stunning night.
In my mind, an alloy is ultimately practical *because*, as you commented,
to be hybrid anticipates the future.

You also admitted:
if you only have clay on hand, then from clay even the centipede is cast.
I'll add that clay, the result of weathering rocks, is its own betwixt.

A Daughter, After Being Asked If I Write the *Occasional Poem*

After leaving Raxruhá, after
crossing Mexico with a coyote,
after reaching at midnight
that barren New Mexico border,
a man and his daughter
looked to Antelope Wells
for asylum and were arrested. After
forms read in Spanish
to the Mayan-speaking father,
after a cookie but no water, after
the wait for the lone bus
to return for their turn, after boarding,
after the little girl's temperature spiked,
she suffered two heart attacks,
vomited, and stopped breathing. After
medics revived the seven-year-old
at Lordsburg station, after
she was flown to El Paso where she died,
the coroner examined
the failed liver and swollen brain. Then,
Jakelin's chest and head were stitched up
and she returned to Guatemala
in a short white coffin
to her mother, grandparents,
and dozens of women preparing
tamales and beans to feed the grieving.
In Q'eqchi', *w-e* means *mouth*.

Brain Fever

(2014)

[Things that make one's stomach churn]
  from *The Pillow Book* by Sei Shōnagon

the reverse side of a brocade

the inside of a cat's ear

newborn mice, hairless and pink, squirming from their nest

the seam of an as-yet-unlined leather robe

a dingy dark recess

a homely woman tending to her sizable brood

a woman who has been sick for a spell—she must strike
her lover, especially if he is not that caring toward her,
as distasteful

[Kimiko's Clipping Morgue: BRAIN file]

BRAIN: "In Pursuit of a Mind Map, Slice by Slice"

BRAIN behavior: see *SHAME, DISTRUST, OCD/neurotransmitters, Rapunzel syndrome,* etc.

BRAIN misc.: "Flame First, Think Later: New Clues to E-Mail Misbehavior"; sealed manila envelope labeled *her vitals*

BRAIN memory: "Memory Implant Gives Rats Sharper Recollection"; "No Memory, but He Filled in the Blanks"; "Researchers Create Artificial Memories in the Brain of a Fruitfly"; photo of Rei tottering on sandy path as Miya runs toward me, the camera—scribbled on back, *girls' first summer on Fire Island*

BRAIN PAN: [empty]

BRAIN DRAIN: [empty]

BRAIN and head syn.: attic, bean, belfry, brain box, conk, dome, noddle, noodle, gray matter

BRAIN dreams (see *DREAM THEORY*)

BAIN [sic], *origin Old English* bana, *thing causing poison* (see *DUPLICITY*)

[file without label]: *Spirit Photograph Exhibit/admit two,* lavender lace thong, two flattened Chinese handcuffs

BRAIN fever: . . . . 2. *a medical condition where a part of the brain becomes inflamed and causes symptoms that present as fever. The terminology is dated, and is encountered most often in Victorian literature, where it typically describes an illness brought about by a severe emotional upset.*

BRAIN poetry: Blake, "Mad Song"; Dickinson, "I felt a Funeral, in my Brain"; Poe, "The Haunted Palace"; Jeffers, "Apology for Bad Dreams"; Anne Sexton, "Angel of Flight and Sleigh Bells"

BRAIN Shakespeare: "these paper bullets of the brain," "In this distracted globe," "dagger of the mind," "Raze out the written troubles of the brain," "memory, the warder of the brain."

BRAIN split (see *CONSCIOUSNESS*, see *WIFE*)

Alarm

> Before doctors learn how it is that the brain's lights turn on, they may have to
> know a lot more about what's happening when the lights are off.
>
> —Benedict Carey

In her dark she surveys empty: the vanity
from the in-laws' Bronx apartment,

the brooch from a lover,
loafers by a coat tree, trench coat,

the husband's profile, an alarm
for news and forecast. Here
                          she appraises fidelity
before the light violates.

The Dream of a Little Occupied Japan Doll

Among the hundred porcelain figurines,
the first one—with slanted eyes, fat cheeks,

queue (though that's Chinese) and Chinese bonnet—
is my favorite. Among all those in pajamas

or gowns or the two in kimono,
the first is my favorite. Of those with rickshaw,

fan, parasol or piccolo—
I keep the first one on my bureau

though she—or he—is not doing a darn thing.
Here in sleep, rivalry is reserved.

And as dreams "tune the mind for conscious awareness"
perhaps this favoritism suggests

I've quit hoarding and now collect myself.

The Dream of Parsnips

Do I wish for a box of cigars—or dynamite?
Do I wish for the sudden squirming of earthworms?

Do I wish for the literal in Grandma Ida's dining room
or some prix fixe? Do I wish for

the standing-outside-his-lit-office-window-at-two-in-the-morning
as only a sophomore can stand . . . or for

the husband to scrap the skank?
Or perhaps for the researcher herself who believes:

"dreaming is not a parallel state but consciousness itself,

in the absence of the senses' input"?
Considering various explanatory projects,

I do wish that wishing would process
whatever calls up an object so white and duplicitous.

The Dream of Bubbles

The unborn "may be 'seeing' something
long before the eyes ever open"—later

making sense of Mr. Bubble or bubbly with an alum
and why I can't visit the museum's

giant squid and whale diorama. Also

the reason I can't open my eyes in pool or pond

to witness the weight of loan.
And why I can't bear the chatter of toddlers

as if sinking to the bottom of a basin. Can I burst
through the transparent?

After all, "the developing brain draws on innate,

biological models of space and time."
Fear blue, fear green, stay clear of aquamarine.

The Dream of a Pillow

Zealous mother or breast,
zealous marshmallow, zealous feathers.

Although the neuroscientist

does not declare, *so what*—
she does believe the brain

observes prop and scene
in a lucid watchfulness

which may play out in proverb or verse
or be utterly meaningless.

Zealous codeine. Zealous noose.

The Dream of a Letter Opener in the Shape of a Mermaid

Tell me which ocean is warmest,

tell me which shore is closest,
tell me which ship tosses trash and which plays a waltz

and how many bottles you've collected
containing messages from shipwrecks.

Is this figure playing in my mind
an unconscious desire or archetypal theme

or are these explanations merely "predetermined ideas,"

assumptions made theory—?
Not wishing to jam the round peg in that square

I also don't wish to submit to
        gastrointestinal or neurological pleasures:
tell me about the sister in a glass case,

a monkey's body glued to that of a fish.

The Dream of Knife, Fork, and Spoon

I can't recall where to set the knife and spoon.
I can't recall which side to place the napkin

or which bread plate belongs to me. Or
how to engage in benign chatter.

I can't recall when more than one fork—
which to use first. Or what to make of a bowl of water.

I can't see the place cards or recall any names.
The humiliation is impressive. The scorn.

No matter how much my brain "revises" the dinner

to see if the host was a family member—
I can't recall which dish ran away with which spoon.

The Dream of a Lacquer Box

I wish I knew the contents and I wish the contents
Japanese—

like hairpins made of tortoiseshell or bone
though my braid was lopped off long ago,

like an overpowering pine incense
or a talisman from a Kyoto shrine,

like a Hello Kitty diary-lock-and-key,
Hello Kitty stickers or candies,

a netsuke in the shape of a squid,
ticket stubs from *A Double Suicide*—

or am I wishing for Mother? searching for Sister?
just hoping to bestow *something Japanese* on my daughters?

then again, people can read anything into dreams

and I do as well. I wish I possessed my mother's
black lacquer box though in my dream it was red,

though I wish my heart were cóntent.

The Dream of Shoji

How to say *milk*? How to say *sand, snow, sow,*

linen, cloud, cocoon, or *albino*?
How to say *page* or *canvas* or *rice ball*?

Trying to recall Japanese, I blank out:

it's clear I know forgetting. Mother, tell me
what to call that paper screen that slides the interior in?

"A French explorer named Michel Siffre lived in a cave for two months, cut off from [daily] rhythms [and emerged] convinced that he had been isolated for only 25 days."

Dust in nostrils
Dust in the dark
Dank clothes, dank *omamori*, moist walls, sludge underfoot—
Sneakers
Tubers?
The word *tubers* and the thought of tubers
Hunger pangs—O Twinkies! O Nachos! O Snickers!
Sneakers
(Never finished that class on Plato when I holed up at a boyfriend's—only to
    find him hollow)
Dust in hair, under fingernails
Dank harness
(I loved Jarrell's *Bat-Poet* because I had no friends either—)
Bats
My sister's watch, no longer coherent

The Dream of a Fire Engine

Without the sun filtering through closed eyelids,
without the siren along the service road,

without Grandpa's ginger-colored hair,
Mother's lipstick, Daughter's manicure,

firecrackers, a monkey's ass, a cherry, Rei's lost elephant,
without past tense, deficit or communist,

without Mao's favorite novel about a chamber,
or the character seeing her own chopped-off feet dancing in fairy slippers,

or the siren with a prof at a hot-sheet-motel—

the scientist of sleep has claimed
that without warm blood a creature cannot dream.

The Dream of Leaves

How to access the material
of the unborn or the infant dream?

To rate, say, a rustling?

To value leaves rustling
before one realizes leaves? Before

one knows what a homonym is
or that every one thing

is a homonym after crowning—

"[Some psychologists say] the findings support the philosopher Martin Heidegger's observation that time 'persists merely as a consequence of the events taking place in it.'"

Water breaks

Rain on the windshield during Braxton Hicks

Caesarean

Commencement

Standing in line for theater tickets to see *Metamorphosis*

Mother is always nearby with things. Pillows. Hot-water bottle. She loves her infant granddaughter more than she loves anyone, even me. And I love that.

Clutching a baby on one hip, a ladle in the other hand.

Do you recall me cooking? I can barely recall what I threw together. Yet you girls have grown to be so striking—

Standing in line at 4 am to get her into the good kindergarten—that was their father—

Standing at the checkout, a child sobbing in the cart for bubble gum

Commencement. The Gulf.

A girl! A girl!

Commencement

Crowning

A Bowl of Spaghetti

"To find a connectome, or the mental makeup of a person,"
researchers experimented with the neurons of a worm

then upgraded to mouse hoping to
"unravel the millions of miles of wires in the [human] brain"

that they liken to "untangling a bowl of spaghetti"

of which I have an old photo: Rei in her high chair intently
picking out each strand to mash in her mouth.

Was she two? Was that sailor dress from Mother?
Did I cook that sauce from scratch? If so, there was a carrot in the pot,

as Mother instructed and I'll never forget
                                        no matter which strand
determines ardor as a daughter's verdict.

Cherry Stems

I'm not too happy that fruit flies have brains

since I swat them whenever I see them or think I see them.
I know about their brains because I met a scientist

who tinkers with their "learning circuitry,"
"the actual mechanics

of how a memory trace is laid down in a nerve cell or neuron."

All this proxy—dissecting the behavior of an insect—
to figure out how the brain works

for something like typing at which my mother was a pro

and me, fairly miserable because of some disorder
which it seems my daughter has inherited

since she also exhibits left/right confusion. However,

she can twist a cherry stem into a bow with her tongue
an ability no doubt from an ancestral brain

but which also reveals something about a summer in Florence.
In other words, too-much-information regarding memory trace.

In a baby

wiring allows

wiring

From our lumpy pullout in the front room
that faced car alarms, hookers calling up to the neighbor

to buzz-me-in-baby, dawn-breaking garbage trucks,
and a boom box in the busted-up park—

I also knew a thumping in the far room:

our infant on her back in the crib
banging her feet on her mattress, realizing

just who jiggled the zebras circling
above her face, a beatific light bulb.

this huge surge ██████████████████

████████████████████████████

████████████████████████████████ is

████████████████████████████

████████████ a kind of ██████████

██████████████████████████████

██████████████████████████████

██████████ host ████████████████

████████████████████████████

Waves sweep under the house pilings,

shoving sand and debris, scumming bikes with salty grit.
Each night, the husband's erratic blood

pumps rivalry into his ribcage. A short-lived glacier,
I'm told. A spike in her fever. In voltage as well—

you know, the need to protect wire from a thunderbolt
striking across school yard then marriage

then one's child's childhood.
Warring factions. Tribes. Bring the soldiers home.

Home is where the surge is.

"Yet the sensation of passing time can be very different. Dr. Zauberman said, 'depending on what you think about, and how.'"

Tweezing eyebrows and thinking about refinancing the mortgage

Tweezing eyebrows and mulling over a daughter's curfew

Baking biscuits and not thinking (was I sixteen?)

While tweezing, I think to use the pressure cooker for the New Year's *sekihan*.

Riding in a train to visit my sister, I recall telling her to be quiet every night
   of our childhood (*I'm so sorry*).

Sorrow

As her father drove her to flute lessons, she kept talking so he wouldn't ask
   what she was up to.

Tweezing eyebrows while fuming over the lice outbreak

Fuck it. Five minutes left of the test, she fills in the remaining bubbles.

Riding in the train to see him, the heat blasting the seat and the vibration
   arousing—

He loved researching penny dreadfuls at the Forty-Second Street Library.
   Cranking the rolls of microfilm—

Rebooting

Googling *Syria*.

Tweezing, I recall last night: our pulses flashed in the slant of streetlight
   across the bed.

Balls

Prince and coach. Coach and batter.

Cookie dough. Clay. Stick.
Bearings. Gum. Spit.

Have one—
but know that apart from nature

a sphere may indicate "human artifacture,"

a mark of handiwork.
Mandala, lotus throne, rose window. Wax.

Hula hoop mimics halo
while in his sleep my husband dodges so often

my head keeps spinning.

(Then there's Miss Molly
and what she sure likes best of all—)

The Secret Lives of Planets

lines lifted from "Now in Sight: Far-Off Planets," Dennis Overbye

whether the bodies are really planets or failed stars—
the first team spied a pair of dots about four billion miles out—
telescope mirrors are jiggled and warped—

"Every extrasolar planet detected so far has been a wobble"—
swaddled in large disks of dust, the raw material of worlds—
the bodies are really planets or failed stars—

"Kepler himself would recognize [how they follow] his laws of orbital motion"—
fuzzy dots moving slightly around from exposure to exposure—
jiggled and warped—

three planets circle a star known as HR 8799 in constellation Pegasus—
The problem seeing other planets is picking them from the glare of parent stars—
or failed stars—

giant planets in the outer reaches, [leave] plenty of room
for smaller ones to lurk undetected in the warmer inner regions—
whether parents are really failed stars—
telescopic, mirrored, and warped—

Likeness

In his book on writing poetry, *The Triggering Town*, Richard Hugo wrote, "O.K. I'm just fooling around." I often think of that statement as advice. And I thought of it again when a friend and I exchanged writing prompts on Zoom. After a few minutes of scribbling, we mostly talked about how we create prompts so differently: she, reading a poem and trying her hand at something like the poem's syntax. Me, using the prompt as a jumping off point. To access one's raw material. But mostly to, yeah, fool around.

Go ahead—I laugh—*send me a grip of blazons.*

Prompt

Five things that are in your grandmother's handbag

Five things that remind you of Chutes-and-Ladders

Five things that make you panic

Five words you can never spell

Five things you know are ghosts

Survival

Like zombie bees or *zombees*   *—not really zombie bees—*   I am
not really a monster.
                    What appears as monstrous behavior   is actually
due to *a fly egg*   deposited inside said bee
                    that hatches then alters   the little bee's little brain

although   funnily enough   the freakish   nocturnal behavior
          favors the bee's continued survival.

Well, me, too: survival   can be traced to
          the interspecific   and her name is Bingo

Unforgiving

Like   the snow leopard—

                              the *mysterious existence*   *deduced*

          from tracks, droppings, and stories—

yes, like   the snow leopard

                              threatened   by her neighbor's

          desire for body parts

                    I conceal myself

Like the snow leopard   I know the terrain

          in which I abide   is   *unforgiving*

Virulent

Unlike the Emerald Ash Borer   I am   not exactly a Far East native
        and   I do cause   *a little trouble*   at home
                        which is not   *a forest*
                    where trees *harvest sunlight*   and *take in water*

but like   the Emerald Ash Borer   when it comes to boring

    my home was also   *tough to digest*   and at times   even   virulent

Lonesome Kimiko

Unlike George, Kimiko was not found on Pinta Island, an island thought to have not one tortoise left;

unlike George, too, Kimiko has never come to recognize Fausto Llerena, the then-72-year-old ranger of said island—in fact, she's never met Don Fausto;

in fact, no one like Don Fausto will ever say of her, "He was like a member of the family to me. To me, he was everything." No one like senior official Washington Tapia will weep and exclaim "it was like losing his grandparents";

unlike George, the last giant tortoise of his subspecies in this archipelago, Kimiko's death will not represent the extinction of a creature right before another creature's eyes;

unlike George, Kimiko will never be on display, postmortem, in a museum.

Like George, however, a few people do *ooh* and *ahh* over Kimiko, for which she feels eternally special (though not as in "species");

and Kimiko would count herself fortunate if in her usual morning spot when she dies: a hot shower with the radio on to girl-group songs;

yes, like Lonesome George, Kimiko has always been lonesome. Also like him, she has not been very often alone. Unlike him, finally, there will be others— extinct tortoises that is.

The Moss Piglet

Kimiko considers *the morphology of cryptic species* a funny thing: she
would've assumed the tardigrade a fairly singular creature (though there
are the nicknames *moss piglet* and *water bear*) and yet over a thousand *have
been described* (though perhaps not all named)—

though perhaps not so astounding since they're found in hot springs, under
polar ice, and,

most conveniently, on lichen or moss. Or soil. Or marine or freshwater
sediment. So sure—why not fifty bajillion names depending on
idiosyncrasies! For the record,

the Phylum is *barrel-shaped* with four pairs of legs, each pair having claws
known as *disks,*

—useful for reproduction when eggs are laid inside *a shed* then covered
by sperm so fourteen days later *wahlah!* (as Kimiko's mother would say).
Although none needs a mate, *usually.* Which would have been convenient for
someone like Kimiko who has married three times instead of leaving well
enough alone—

at any rate, a tardigrade (*tardy-grade*) resembles an inflated spacesuit or a
vacuum cleaner nozzle or a manatee fetus without eyes. *Cute!*

Not surprising to Kimiko is that they're all cuter than Kimiko!

But, returning to taxonomy, if Kimiko ever discovers a tardigrade, she
will call it *Kimiko*— though she'll never be the most resilient animal of her
species.

Toying

[Tiddlywinks]

Unlike *Tiddlywinks*, I do not move if pressed. Especially by a squidger. Like *Tiddlywinks*, I am strategic (develop, maintain, break—i.e., DMB). Especially squopping an opponent. In particular after I turned thirty and did not feel compelled to tolerate winks and such. I do, however, delight in feeling felt.

[Mouse Trap]

Like *Mouse Trap*, I *can* keep my little trap shut. Chiefly when it comes to girlfriends' ailments or affairs. (Not so much my own youthful escapades.) Just don't call me *mousey*.

[Doll-E-Drink 'n' Wet Set's miniature evenflo]

Petite as I am, I am not miniature-sized like the *Doll-E-Drink 'n' Wet Set*'s teensy *evenflo*. And I will never be completely empty. Even if you—yes, *you*—leave me prone and alone.

Learning from a Murder

Unlike crows, Kimiko does not *noisily congregate around dead comrades*, nor does she *mob corpse-bearing volunteers*, although she knows darn well that some choose to do so.

Unlike crows, Kimiko cannot *always tell individual humans apart by their faces.* This has frustrated Jay, although he's been slipping up himself as of late.

Unlike crows, Kimiko does not *divebomb* anyone.

Unlike crows, Kimiko probably does not *leave a strong impression on dead crows.*

Unlike crows, Kimiko is human and aware there are other creatures besides humans or a murder that *pays attention to its dead*

including *chimpanzees, elephants, dolphins, and relatives of crows known as scrub jays.*

(Scrub jays!)

Unlike crows, Kimiko saw her mother for the last time in a pine coffin at the Pleasantville Funeral Home where the director, thinking it a compliment, remarked that *Orientals never look their age.*

Like crows, the presence of the dead can tell those of the same species *to pay careful attention as a way of gathering information about threats . . . a long-term learning opportunity,*

and she is also a scare and doesn't enjoy "eating crow." Further,

a dead pigeon [has] no effect on Kimiko and she doesn't believe in any gods, per se.

Toxic Flora

(2010)

In her comments on the manuscript, Jill felt that the three zuihitsu overwhelmed (my word, not hers) the lyric poems. She suggested excerpting from one of them and spreading the paragraphs throughout. And she was so right. I tried the one on sexual cannibalism:

Nowadays when friends read about Darwin and something like *sexual cannibalism*, they immediately expect a poem. Then there's my own jealousy of the material itself: that someone will get to it first. Whichever the pressure, that the female mantis "devours the head of the still-mating male and then moves on to the rest of his body" is a shocking bit of information. Because I am past childbearing years? Because I have daughters? Or because it just seems vulgar to eat in bed?

Nepenthe

Quaff, oh quaff this kind nepenthe, . . .

—Edgar Allan Poe

The *Nepenthes rafflesiana,* or pitcher plant,
a bowl-shaped leaf with liquid at bottom,

acts like an animal predator to attract then digest insects
such as the itinerant ant that scouts around *the dry lip*

then bids colony members follow only to slip inside
owing to increased humidity or nectar secretion.

Scientists measure this completely passive phenomenon

using tiny electrical probes leading me to wonder—
just what is the reward for such studies?

botanical insights? lessons on symbiosis or unpredictability?

For me, more than the thought of wet lips
or Homer who mentioned Nepenthe

as a potion to dispel one's misery,

I think of memorizing poetry in the fourth grade:
Edgar Allan Poe, while longing to forget *the lost Lenore,*

composed verse after verse that implanted recollection.
That drug, that conductivity,

that pleasurable sensation of stumbling into memory.

Toxic Flora

There is something vital
about *Passiflora auriculata,*

which for over a million years has varied its cyanogens

to discourage feasting insects

although the *Heliconius* butterfly
resolutely adapted to those same poisons

finally transmuting itself into one—

actually repelling predators
as it leisurely fluttered

from leaf to blossom
seeking out a haven for eggs.

What does this demonstrate about toxins
or residence?

Or carrying around the childhood home
where the father instructs the daughter

on the uses of poison then
accuses her of being so potent?

On Deceit as Survival

Darwin could not believe an insect

would visit a blossom that had no reward
and insisted that the green-winged orchid

must withhold its nectar deep inside.
But he was deceived as well

since this orchid does not offer nectar

in its own Darwinian-desire
to attract then rid itself of the useful bee.

Still others smell like feces or carrion

for the sort that prefers
to lay eggs in such environs.

Yet another species resembles

a female bumble bee,
ending in frustrated trysts—

or appears to be two fractious males
which also attracts—no surprise—

a third curious enough to join the fray.
What to make of highly evolved Beauty

bent on deception as survival?

And how can a mother instruct on deceit
when girls so readily flaunt thigh and thong?

and parking lots are replete
with the preternatural buzz of a car alarm?

Demeter's Cuttings

My own Mother taught me suspicion:
to question a man's gifts, whether truffles or trifles.

She also taught me the names of trees
and how to rub off

the dried sheaths on silver dollar stalks
then toss the seeds back over the bed.

She didn't teach me much else, and truthfully
I like nature—not to tend but visit,

to watch it take care of itself.
Still, a fist full of snapdragons—

a flock of yellow dragonflies—

a cluster of cicada nymphs—

this is what I wish to entice my daughter back to:
what I love to what I love

while below, the subway quakes the whole building.
*
Once she called to tell me, *Mother, don't make me choose.*

A young man had taken her into the subway
to his parents' home for dinner

and by curfew she called to say there were no cabs in sight.

I said, *You're too young to stay with him.*

And I imagined him standing over her
as she covered the receiver, saying—

My mother won't let me stay.

(Where was the father? Teaching his new wife's son to piss in a pot?)
*
What I've learned about men is that they bludgeon
to make a point: that he will not shut up

until his woman weeps and folds in on herself.
Blames herself for his empty hands. Then

he can dismiss her—or hold her—
as if rescuing her from himself. This

is what I learn, daily, to walk away from:

shut up, you're wrong. Who cares. And now

in my own apartment I wait past her curfew
to doze or leaf through *People, Self* or *Us*;

listen to restaurant crowds dispersing,
the drunks heaving below my window;

wait up to hear a car door. I know

that first boy takes a turbulent daughter
to keep her in the dark

but I still wait for keys at the door.

Was she so bored in these rooms cluttered
with scarves and cosmetics? A few African violets?

And isn't that all right—to be a child and be bored?
*
My own childhood was a doll

that could do nothing but close her eyes,

games with nothing but dice and "men,"
a tape recorder to record—what? That boredom?
*
Then there were records of myths and *Peter Pan.*

The marsh across the street.
Cattails. Jack-in-the-pulpits.

And trees so high you couldn't climb them, or

if you did, the jays would peck your head
to protect their squawky nests.

Then there was the odd heron.
Then there was her father.
*

Before she met this young man, I asked,
Do you miss me when we're apart?

and she answered, *I miss myself, Mommy.*
These days she claims, *I'll do what I want.*

*

In spite of the blue porcelain cups,
the kittykat clock hung on the wall, its tail ticking—

there comes a point
when the mother must risk losing her daughter

by telling her, *No, you must leave him tonight.*

My own sisters tell me, *She'll come home.*
And when she does, the morning glory vine

on the construction fencing across the street
will open its pink lyric.

Then we'll toast bread and perk coffee

and arrange the asphodel on the yellow table.

Or will she regard the welt on her arm
as an exotic flower from that other world—

I cannot say.

Brooding

Misinformation lasts millennia. As when a student
hauling a trawl bucket from the black mid-waters off Monterey

found a mass of squid eggs with the mother beside them—

surely a coincidence
since the female squid abandons her eggs.

Then a year later, another bucket produced the same—
this time hatchlings—though disbelief persisted.

But when a scientist lowered a robot with camera and lights

he spied a female cradling several thousand eggs
and waving her tentacles to aerate and nourish.

Misconceptions about squid arose
because the deep is so poorly explored.

And because one might substitute one's fear
for hard evidence. Especially with regard to mothering.

My own daughters declare,
If you'd been around more, we'd have gone mad—

which is somehow comforting. Cuttlefish
are next under scrutiny.

A reservoir of Dickinson's slant rhyme

week, work, back, thick
[comb], scene, on; corn, noon; sun, gone; alone, bone
slant, delight
life, belief; abyss, [twice], consciousness; place,
    [consciousness], face
not, felt; pain, men
denomination, classifying; affair, are
obscuring, intuitions; well, unplausible

Just Walk Away Renee

The mite harvestman, a daddy longlegs

found in 400-million-year-old fossils,

has wandered across several continents
without so much as a swim. A conundrum

if it weren't for plate tectonics,

a notion only realized in 1911
when a scientist matched up fossils

on either side of the Atlantic.
I think about this discovery and try to tease out a simile

but really, it's just better to leave
the first land animals alone. The shifting

and colliding and breaking apart alone.

The drifting. The sadness—
that marks the opening of a quest

only to discover estrangement.

A fistful of stress.
A palm of psalms.

A coatroom of cadence.

Yellow Jackets—

protect through venom and candor.

While timing their own picnics
to mother's tray, father's tongs,

or baby's saucer-sized cheeks,

they can sting intruders repeatedly
unlike the honeybee's suicidal sortie.

I like that. I like X
who calls people out at brunch

through simple narration:
your mouth never stops moving.

Or, *you eat off other plates as if they're your own.*

Or, *you check your Blackberry when no one is talking about you.*

Or, *you laugh whenever you insult someone.*

A startling attribute I wish I could emulate
if only my sting possessed such integrity.

Awareness

Among the burrowing owl's
scraps of carpet and tinfoil

tucked into the humid straw,
the hoard of cow dung is especially prized

as it attracts dung beetles.

The owls watch for hours
revealing a tool of attraction

of which those clever creatures

may not be aware.
What then *is* awareness?

Connecting shit to consequence:
the flicker that links, say,

chlorine to climax—
or who consumed whom at faculty picnics.

Big Feathered Hats

worn by women a century ago
necessitated aligning the body in a threshold

just so. It's this *just so*

that intrigues Professor Iriki,
who has probed clumps of tissue

to uncover how cells and circuits

map the world around it

to the body's schema.
To sense that tight spot

whether concrete
or like the night her lover admitted

he'd had an affair with his own mother—
his word, *affair*—

and she knew in her bones
which was really her brain

that she should get the fuck out.
Those feathers. That exit.

Pinguinus Impennis

Large, flightless, and defenseless,
the great auk was captured
for feathers for featherbeds—
hunters loosening the plumage in cauldrons
fueled with the oil from
the freshly killed auks before them.
After the 1830 volcanic eruption in Iceland, after
museums and collectors vied for the skins
belonging to *the penguins of the North*,
in 1844, the last pair was beaten to their deaths
and their solitary egg dashed on the rocks of Eldey Island.
Could we not sleep on straw or goose down?
What dreams are worth such extinction?
And are they dreams I'd wish to own?

Cyanopsitta Spixii

Every skin that remained of the Spix's macaw
evidenced a death in captivity
and a history usurped by farmers and trappers
among the trees of inland Brazil.
How extreme to be so prized
that price kept one's species faint
until a single male remained in those forests.
Attempts to foster regeneration
by introducing a once-captive female
were never successful: the survivor
was last seen saving his fascination
for a macaw of another species. In the wild
bewilderment happens to the point of oblivion—
I know myself.

Sedna

Come to find out, Sedna
is the Inuit woman,

whose father cast her from their kayak,
thus transforming her into the spirit of the sea—

but also the name of 2003 VB12,

a planet or something beyond Pluto.
It is the first body to be discovered

in the Oort Cloud, *a hypothetical region
of icy objects that become comets.*

But questions remain: how
can a region be hypothetical?

how can a scientist not know

what a planet is? how could a father
throw his daughter from a kayak

even if she did write poetry
that hurt his feelings?

I am not sorry.
He always said, *art comes first.*

But that is a murky region

for fathers and daughters—
what comes first.

And what my daughters wish to know is
did she drown for his sake

or to learn how depths betray?

Refuse

Scientists now observe that Saturn's largest moon

boasts a substantial orange atmosphere
and is inscrutable to the human eye.

Will their spinning camera detect lakes
of liquid methane? Regions of ice water?

What we do know is that Saturn

(not the one with rings of ice and rock)

ate his children rather than die in supreme betrayal;

that it is difficult to see things
from the child's vantage

though one was previously a child.
This makes me sad.

And I wonder about surface features—
the dark and light craters

seen with unprecedented clarity.

The mostly pure ice.

The fields of clouds.
Or children turning into orbiting debris,

I think that fathers think.

My Very Exciting Magic Carpet Just Sailed Under Nine Palace Elephants

Before the recent conference on Pluto's status
a planet appeared beyond number nine, not to be seen again.

Since then, Pluto's been demoted
from full-fledged to *dwarf planet*;

and a planet, heretofore undefined,

is *any object in orbit around the Sun
that is dominant in its immediate neighborhood—*

though from my viewpoint
if a body is not considered a planet

then it shouldn't be called *a dwarf planet.*
It should have its own category altogether.

(Maybe *rockette*
since scientists are so enamored of female names.)

Thankfully, we needn't wait for the definition of a dwarf planet—
something about *self-gravity, rigid body forces,* and *planetesimals.*

But what in the world is a *planetesimal*
and how to mourn the loss of my *Elegant Mother*?

Icebreaker

Scientists, unnerved by stretches of melted ice
around the North Pole,

cannot discern whether the pace of change
is mostly greenhouse gas or natural influence

missed in earlier forecasts.

Shipping magnates and drillers of oil
are *not displeased* for the now-watery sea routes

and care less that polar bears scavenge
to eat and reproduce. Ice retreat?

Ice deficit? Thawing permafrost?
Artic Oscillation?

That we cannot care beyond filling a gas tank
or wondering if a summer patio will be under water

may be the ironic side effect
of evolutionary biology. Or just plain narcissism.

Or just plain laziness or laxness.

Or just plain greed.
Or just plain brainlessness.

Or just plain lack of imagination.
That Arctic sinkhole.

. . . As I scribble and revise, I want to further how I can use repetition to create expectation then swerve for sparks and psychological play. Resonance can create a sensory-based poetics versus one of melodramatic *sighing*. Decades of considering poetic closure have led me to this view of craft. To aim for a physically informed poetics. Everything conspires in closure. *Yes?*

Maude

Although the exoplanet Gliese 436 b
orbiting around Gliese 436

may possess a livable zone
in between its fixed-sunny and -frigid sides,

it does not possess a more transcendent name.

I'd like to know as much as anyone
if this exoplanet possesses an atmosphere

but more, I'd like my daughter
to watch for the wobbles

that a planet's gravity creates
in the motion of its stars

and name these masses after family members:

Kimiko would be ideal—
but really, I'm thinking *Maude*.

Planet Maude.

Matching Maude's qualities to a celestial body would be to suggest
the obvious attributes

a daughter has identified in her mother,

my mother. But rather than be obvious
I could take pleasure in naming any planet after her—

though, if pressed,
I imagine one that is petite, habitable, remote,

and owning a number of moons.

An atmosphere surely.

There was a short time I wanted the same daughter

to go into mycology—
to name a fungus

after the men in the family.
I don't think either would be asking too much.

From a prompt to reuse the last line from another draft

The air cannot feel the air
The windstorm cannot feel the storm
The snowstorm cannot feel the snow
The whirlwind cannot feel the whirl
The hailstorm cannot feel the hail/hale
The twister cannot feel the twist
The hurricane cannot feel the hurry
The dust devil neither dust nor devil
The monsoon cannot feel the soon
The cyclone cannot feel alone
The draft cannot assume the raft

The Sweetwater Caverns

Curious to see the caverns,
we detoured in Tennessee
to ramble through Fat Man's Misery,
past a ballroom and gun powder machine
till we reached The World's Second Largest Underground Lake—
on which my husband had promised a ride
in a glass-bottom boat.

There, a kid hunched over a hot-rod magazine.
Dan, I think his name was,
radiant, in clammy, artificial light.

I asked Dan, *college-break?*
He nodded inside his hoodie
then helped me into the glass-bottom hold.
I peered into the milky water
and watched the seeded trout swim up for the chum
he dumped overboard on our account.

He was milky white himself,
from months of cave sitting.

I wondered if he'd write a poem
on a summer spent underground.
Thought to suggest it—how foolish—
then wondered if what I really wanted was Dan,

as I stepped into his boat, to take my arm and ask me something—

at this middle age, probably for a couple coins
then give promise of safe passage
as he ferried me to the realm of the dead

that I've been thinking about for several years
not because of a girlfriend's cancer
but because my body is no longer young.
I mean, lovely—
and that there's no turning back to that water's edge.

There's only the couch
every afternoon at four o'clock
and not wanting to ever move. Not wishing to die exactly—
just not wanting to rise
because the light feels so pressured. And I can't have
that ardent glow reflected back while brushing teeth
or fastening a necklace. Now there's this

casting around for other stuff—
the daughters' secrets—the pathetic urge to write about their secrets—

or a crush on Charon. Not an old man as it turns out
but a youth, colorless and tired of his iPod.

No, he's not really of interest to me.
And this is my secret: that I wish he were—
as with those arms
reaching through clouds of cigarette smoke
to lead me into reeking dives.

I'm past that. And he, Dan,
not the poetic Charon—
will probably climb out of the caverns
into the six o'clock evening sun. Stretch. Change his shirt,
eat his mother's meatloaf and head off in a rusted Honda
for the Piggly Wiggly parking lot
with a six-pack and a girl,

those hand-sized moths flitting in the light
as the sheriff chases the kids to another dead-end spot—

those enormous dusty moths my husband caught
for me to hold in my hand
because he knows, in the afternoon light after the dank caverns,
how fluttery the furry wings will feel.
Which is more than melodrama can bear.

To have wished for Dan *to ask me something?*
I know *the passage* is not what you wanted to hear.

The Search for Names

The right to name Planet X belonged to the Lowell Observatory
where the Kansas farm boy engaged

to photograph the night heavens using a blink comparator

quickly suggested *Slipher*, after his superior.
The widow, Constance Lowell, suggested *Zeus, Lowell,* and *Constance*.

Then eleven-year-old Venetia Burney
put forward *Pluto,* ruler of the underworld

(as well a dark and cold terrain)
and a god who could turn invisible.

She was eating breakfast with her grandfather, Falconer Madan,
when he read about the search in the dailies.

Lucky girl. Fortunate planet. Exultant netherworld.

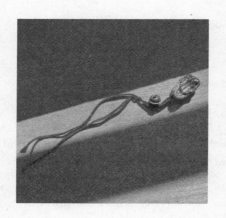

The Narrow Road to the Interior
(2006)

On the first page of Bashō's *The Narrow Road to the Interior*, he wrote: *By nightfall, we reached Sōka, my bony shoulders sore from the heavy pack. Though I intended to take nothing, I needed a washi jacket for the night chill, a yukata, rain gear, brush and inkstone. There was also the added weight from farewell gifts that I could hardly leave behind.*

I cobbled together this translation from the editions collected over the decades. *The Narrow Road to a Far Province* (Dorothy Britton) is my copy from grad school, and then *The Narrow Road through the Provinces* (Earl Miner), *The Narrow Road to the Deep North* (Nobuyuki Yuasa), *The Narrow Road to Oku* (Donald Keene), *Back Roads to Far Towns* (Cid Corman and Kamaike Susumu), *The Narrow Road to the Interior* (Sam Hamill), *The Narrow Road through the Hinterlands* (Steven D. Carter), and *Bashō's Narrow Road* (Hiroaki Sato). Howard sent me a PDF of his own walk on that pilgrimage route: "On the Trail of a Ghost" in the February 2008 *National Geographic*. I recently found a copy in a secondhand bookshop.

Interesting that in the West, journals are regarded as records of travel, which is not necessarily so in Japan. Veracity was the case in the journals of Bashō's disciples, but not in the master poet's *The Narrow Road to the Interior*. I mean, *was* his jacket made from washi?

April 2023 note to self: Now that "The Zuihitsu and the Toad-stool" is out in the world, I need to reconsider what "barn door" I opened with that first attempt, "The Downpour," written for The Poetry Project's millennial celebration of Sei. How many of my own attempts were really informed by "Paterson"? I'll have to see what Jan and Nicole have to say.

(How else to write about a safe deposit box, file cabinet, lacquer bentobako?)

I thought my Narrow Road would be my exploration, not models for others to follow.

The Narrow Road—scattered tanka, i.

At low tide the water disappears below the service road and the mud
twitches with seven kinds of crab. Now he can leave but stays.

In a room overlooking pine, I stop thinking of Mother's death and think of
my lover's hands only to recall Mother brushing knots from my hair.

When he lifts a whelk out of the bay, it furls back into the shell. Who wouldn't!

On the answering machine, my daughter's voice reports *I'm not coming
home*. At least she feels these close rooms are home—I whisper to the door.

Yesterday a field of rain. Today, a field of *missed*.

About ocean currents I do not know; but of the gulf in this daughter's heart,
I well recall my own.

About her daughter's whereabouts, she knows enough; but of dragonflies,
she collects books.

Utica Station

Dep. 10:07 a.m. to N.Y. Penn Station

In the cavernous station, the train delayed for over an hour, I have watched a woman tend her newborn. She is tall, slender, has light dark skin and light eyes (green?). She ties her hair back. I cannot see the baby. The man who picked up the ticket and kissed them, very black. Shaved head. I have watched her because her baby is so quiet. And I have not heard her voice.

On the train, she sits one seat ahead and across the aisle. When the train brakes in Albany, the baby cries *ahh!* And she replies, *ahh!* And I think, *just what I would do,* then feel miserable. *Was I* ever so attentive?

Placing one or the other child in the stroller, on the changing table, in a sassy seat, in the sandbox surrounded by plastic starfish and seahorses?

Stay. Come back.

She cradles the child—a boy by the blue?—her rocking, syncopated with the train's chugging. Rain flecks the gray window. We pass a ditch of one hundred tires. A muddy lot of containers. Trees like sticks. A stray willow. We pass by the buds with such speed it could be late winter.

My heart is swollen, large as a newborn.

I do not want to return to their infancies. I would merely do the same: want to be in this notebook, not on the carpet covered with dolls. To be at the window waiting for their father, not swinging them in the park.

That was my mother—in the sandbox.

The farther south, the greener. Is it my imagination—or the proximity to the river?

I see a couple on a tiny jetty, holding a pink blanket.

My heart is swollen. As if a gland, not a muscle.

But I am wrong. There were stories I'd read and reread. *Mike Mulligan and His Steam Shovel. The Runaway Bunny. Ping, the Duck.* If I read "a big word," I'd explain as if the explanation were part of the narrative: *private*, one's very own; *escape*, get away.

There were evenings where we ate a picnic dinner on the Columbia lawns while their father worked late. I remember because when a plane roared over us, I'd say *plane plane* and she would look up to watch it zoom away.

One of my first tasks was to name things. Then it became her task. One daughter's then the next. We'd walk from apartment to park—*Pizza. Doggie. Firetruck*—naming things—*Daisy.*

Train. Bus. Car.

It is so difficult to travel with an infant—the bags of plastic things. One's own pockets, weighted with keys and change. Maybe a magazine stuck in somewhere. Balancing a cup of coffee with one hand, steering the stroller with the other. The baby struggling to be held. Difficult pleasures.

Writing time, remote.

I told myself then, *I need to slow down*—as if picking lice off a child's head. As if reading a poem—instead of sniffing around for the self on some median.

Along this train ride down the Hudson, the tracks run so close to the water it's as if the tracks were laid on pilings. Or as if the water were the rails.

I wonder if there is clay along the river's edge—just as Barbara and I found clay in the brook behind her house. Or as my daughters dug into the sand for the red clay on Fire Island, our hands afterward, cinnabar-red.

Always, *Mommy needs to—I need to—*

I look up from the notebook and see a tiny island with the shell of a castle— what is that? Is that how I've been a mother?

Dogwood blossoms, a cloud in the grove of branches.

A sailboat. A rowboat.

The mother and infant sleep now, the boy like a cat on her chest. Or, as if her heart rested across her sweater. I do recall that lovely pressure.

As we near the GWB, a tugboat towing a barge. Part of the bridge is wrapped in cloth. As if chilled.

I wish we didn't need to plunge into a tunnel.

Now forsythia. Now weeping cherry. I think of my mother, dead these past seven years—eight by Buddhist count.

Come back—

Through a brief tunnel, I can see a boy behind me reflected in the window. He's been kicking my seat as if sport. I need water to swallow an aspirin. I need to stretch.

My heart is swollen, as if—a hot water bottle!

The mother pats the baby's back. With the other hand, she begins to collect jackets for them both.

To put on an infant's jacket, I'd curl my hand through the small cuff and up the sleeve, then pull her arm through. A tiny trick.

There was a difficult moment on a city bus: when I finally got the baby to stop stamping on the seat by plunking her down, the passenger behind me leaned forward and said, *you're a good mother.* I nearly wept.

Stay. Come back.

A mother with a fishing rod.

Looking for sensation on some median. In some station. Now speeding away from an acquaintance, I might have asked, *shall I slip off my dress?* But didn't. There is no longer that urgency.

A mother with a plastic kite.

This is the difference: I can't find myself trailing a man around a room, screening gesture and tone.

This is the difference: I thought I was missing. Missing something.

As if a party balloon.

If my hair didn't get so crushed, I'd wear a baseball cap, too. (What would it say?)

Stay. Come back. Water. Pee-pee. You.

The sudden brick landscape of Harlem. Just before the last tunnel—the dozen poles in the river, swollen and rotted from a long-vanished pier.

That's what the heart was—swollen—like a mother weeping for something. *A pier.*

Appear missing.

Illumination

Point then pronounce
—*bunny   firetruck   ice cream*—
To teach a child a word
A jigsaw piece of dreams

Pulse and Impulse

Black Twig, Rome, Manchurian, Fuji, Gala, Granny Smith, Red Delicious—
Sam, Sylvia, Nelson, Royal Anne, Cashmere, Bing—

January 1st. *I was hoping to walk the dog in the Prospect Park meadow this morning, but the rain was coming down in sheets and she had to be dragged out just to pee. Funny how much she dislikes rain and baths but so readily jumps into messy puddles where possible. As long as it stinks.*

Back in bed I'm reading Louise Glück's Meadowlands. I'm thinking what it means—to find words. "I'm sick of your world / that lets the outside disguise the inside."

What does it mean for a woman to seek models, whether as someone to emulate or resist? And how is the body contained in one's work apart from subject matter?

I began with my own soft but tense body to seek words and a poetic—to seek models who would guide. Mother was a model for the intuitive—which I didn't understand or appreciate until I began to understand my own process—a process of betrayal. The one I trust although I couldn't consciously comprehend her powerful reliance on the unconscious. I don't believe she did either. That to some extent it was cultural.

January 4th. *Appointment with gynecologist this afternoon—PAP smear positive. Which is a negative thing.*

Emily Dickinson, Gertrude Stein, Edna St. Vincent Millay, Elizabeth Bishop, Marianne Moore, H.D.—

I realize now that when mother died in a car accident seven years ago—the girls were four and six, I was thirty-eight—that I had never felt as deeply as when I felt that loss. As though I'd never felt love or loss. And I began to understand missing something I had always missed. Something my mother couldn't give me because no mother can give a child what the mother gives in fairy tales. Which is one thing she did give me—fairy tales. (Perhaps that is where girls learn about the body: Sleeping Beauty, Rapunzel—) Little did I know that my mother was both the mother and stepmother in "Hansel and Gretel."

CJ tells me my inside and outside reside very closely. That is a good thing.

*

January 5th. *I want to write poems that "answer" the quotes I lift from Louise's—even if completely out of context.*

Murasaki Shikibu, Sei Shonagon, Ono no Komachi, Lady Ise—

When deeply unhappy I lie down, cry, feel my whole body ripped open with sorrow. Delicious because it is delicious to feel feelings. As when mother died, I felt relieved to not feel numb but to lie down on the floor and weep.

So, I began with my own soft but tense body to seek words and a poetic—a guide.

The mother and evil stepmother. I accept that.

Models? There's always the Japanese: Murasaki Shikibu's The Tale of Genji *and Sei Shonagon's* The Pillow Book. *Both admired for their daring subject matter, aesthetics, and prose styles. I love Sei Shonagon's "Sympathy Is the Most Splendid of All Qualities." Also, her list of "hateful things."*

I love the sense of abandon.

January 5th continued. *Why do the neighbors allow their dog and toddler to run in the common garden? I am not even sure which one is responsible for digging holes. In the Spring, we will see if any of the bulbs have survived their exuberance. I am glad to hear the cheeriness but sorry to see even this muddy winter patch so worn. My annoyance sounds like the in-laws complaining that the girls always break something whenever we visit. Their busy little hands undoing or accidentally smashing this or that. Their delighted bodies in rooms meant for seated adults.*

The oldest is so full of high spirits—whether thumbing through catalogs for t-shirts and nail polishes or reporting some cliquish crime on the phone or writing a book review—that I sometimes forget how much she needs me. Her increasingly womanly body with a tiny child's face—needs me.

*

January 7th. *I am afraid to call the doctor. Finally afraid. Whenever I walk the dog, I feel I'm a little bit running away from home. The dog and leash are the tether.*

The threshold is not ambiguous here.

Sam, Sylvia, Nelson, Royal Anne, Cashmere, Bing—

January 8th. *Classical Japanese was not my undoing but certainly caused further humiliation. I can still speak Japanese babytalk. I can still teach daughters a few baby words or the words to cue them in Japanese dances: fune (boat), tegami (letter), naku (cry)—I can still feel the dances I learned in high school in my own limbs. They wear my yukata.*

(The folk dances are the same dances we perform every July for the Buddhist festival, for our ancestors. Now we dance them for her.)

With or without fluency, I can still love the zuihitsu as a kind of air current and what arises is very subjective, intuitive, and spontaneous—qualities I trust. Also, a clear voice.

That it was cultivated by a woman and feels significant—as a writing space for women. It is by its own nature a fragmented anything. I love long erratic pieces into which I can thrash around—make a mess. Lose the intellect.

Begin with your own fleshy body to seek fragments that will sustain.

I think of what we are left of Sappho's work—so ravaged by patriarchal flames yet still enduring. Endearing.

I love Keene's phrase "an intriguing sentence or two."

To invite the intellect back in for re-vision.

To feel randomness.

Not obliged to stay with a rational line of thought. I mean—I do not need to compromise a train of thought and, in such a way, can really explore raw material, negative connotations: subjectivity, intuition, irrationality (what a short essay that lacks a formal structure might suggest). What is wrong with subjectivity anyway? My fact. The fact of my experiences.

The doctor told me I need a cone biopsy and because I am not having any more children she will be "aggressive." I felt faint. In her hands she held the drawing of a uterus. I watched her point to the cervix and how much she will cut.

(Seemingly spontaneous. Intentionally random, I should say.)

*

January 9th. *I told a friend a few days later and she said she had a simi-lar procedure a year ago and had also been afraid. I asked her why she didn't tell me, and she said because it isn't something one talks about. Meaning: it's an ambiguous virus, sexually conveyed. I discovered a number of women who have not wanted to talk. Even the gynecologist does not know much—maybe because it isn't lethal to men, and consequently there is little media attention —and a lot of shame.*

There are areas of our life where ambiguity can be lethal. That we explore intuitively.

Intuition, like subjectivity, is not treated as a valid, responsible trait.

Where to cut?

What makes sense? What is not fragmented? What is whole? Obviously if whole, the object embodies potential fragments. And in each fragment, the whole—which, speaking of a poetics founded in mothering, we know from that impossible to pronounce figure of speech, synecdoche.

Where is ambiguity in pleasure and where does it censure?

(I am afraid. And I do not mean to fetishize the fragment. Do not mean to sug-gest the woman's body should be so.)

Irrationality is not valued either. But when working with, for example, jux-taposition, then the rational does not need to be sequential or to fit into a con-ventional framework. The "logic" of a piece may be closer to an "illogical" train of thought—for which of course many have been rewarded. But why not lose the mind—hold it at bay until re-vision.

Celebrate and bathe in these various air currents.

Miya, Rei, Kimi, Tomi—

Paragraphs absorb the emotionality differently than lineated poems. Recently, when I tried rendering a few scribbled paragraphs into conventional poems they did not work; there was an over-sentimentality that was not evident when in blocks. It wasn't that the feeling was camouflaged, more, there was an absorption, an acceptance of the emotion that the verse could not bear. ("Cut-tings" stayed a zuihitsu rather than a series of poems.)

Even in Japanese, the diary subverts the linear by including haiku.
It is lovely when a fragment can be a whole. Not just suggest entirety.
(Or can it?)
Where will she cut? And how much is an aggressive cut?

*

January 11th. *Difficult to wait for results.*

Mother was so intuitive she seemed to disappear at times. As if thinking were less important than trains of thought. Sometimes that disappearing was a way to survive other people's needs, and I imagine to locate her own self. I wish she could have been more present though. My need.

January 12th. *Somewhere there is a note on a Japanese aesthetic value called kaoru, fragrance. I have never been able to find the reference. Do I dare write to a former professor?*

The other ten-year-old girls on Reiko's basketball team are also energetic and unfocused. It must be hormonal. They can barely stand still to listen to the coach. And are also entirely too polite. I'd like to see them get more aggressive with the ball. But when one does jump in the air to swish the ball—how stunning the body.

*

January 13th. *It's my first husband's birthday. Should I send a card? How young we were! How old now this body that lifts free weights three times a week! This body I did not love till after I turned forty—and told myself that whatever is flawed is a flaw—not an issue of, say, chocolate. What to tell my daughters?*

How can the body feel so healthy, look strong—and produce such alarming "results"? The doctor will explore, cut away and scrape sections that look diseased.

How to expose what is hidden? To publish?

Red, Green, Iceberg—

Musk, Sweet, Winter, Wax, Yellow Doll, Honeydew—

January 15th. I know that male philosophers have omitted the body, impure flesh, from their philosophical work on soul, morality, ethics, etc. That women philosophers have begun to insist on the body.

Not just the outside or inside.

January 19th. The youngest doesn't want me to go on a book tour. I gave her a notebook to write to me every day and report what she's done. We held one another. She calmed down.

Dear Reader,
When I first wrote "Sparrow," I regarded the bits of text set off with dingbats as separate sections under the penumbra of its title. I wonder now if the pieces make sense. I think so.

Looking forward,
Kimiko

Sparrow

Bashō wrote—and Sam Hamill translated—*The Moon and Sun are eternal travelers. Even the years wander on.* I always wonder about translations but can never recall enough Japanese to measure a text for myself. So many semesters of bungo and what I recall most is the plodding pace of those semesters in the wood-paneled libraries. Now I rely on translators and have collected five versions.

*

With small children the days pass achingly slow as one pulling her earlobe refuses to nap, the other refuses to sit still unless cartoons tranquilize, but the years speed past. Suddenly, it's true, the three-year-old is thirteen—taller than the mother and recalling the word *no* in numerous forms: *Why should I? I'm going to anyway. Yeah, right.* Even retaining, *No, Mommy.*

Now, with children in this sublet, Saturdays through Tuesdays, I find time has changed. A lover on opposite nights. And the sorrow of flight as I continue to leave my husband; also, the relief, not only of leaving our matched flaws, but from flight itself.

Who is the traveler but the heart—or, depending on the moment, the gut?

A flock, startled by a child's outburst, rises as a single lake of wings.

*

Of the five versions I've collected, one is entitled *The Narrow Road to the Interior*.

*

The dog slinks off my youngest daughter's bed when I enter her room to kiss her goodnight. It's our ritual: the dog hops up at her beckoning, slinks off when I open the door, then when I leave, I hear her quiet flop back on the bed. Flight also includes sleep as this child lies on her back, snores, then rolls over onto her side. Where is she? Only she knows and might not recall the journey upon waking.

Where was the adult before rising too late?

Then, too—legs on my lover's shoulders.

At this moment, it is painful to leave and more painful to stay. Any residue of affection has twisted into an anger keen as a scalpel. Brilliant as a blade. Clean as glass. I wish to hold my husband, hold our *separating*.

> The body would like to recall the humidity even
> or especially in February—
> even as the dogwood too early reddens
> then freezes the next week
> but still is not ruined.
> What of the nestled pupa, more
> uncompromising than we imagine?

*

The brown branches, the pink moments.

I was *at a loss*.

Was marriage my imagination? I look at photos of cheery tanned profiles from little family vacations and cannot know what I was thinking.

*

As after my mother's death, I walk around seeing objects from a haunted world: a child's Easter dress, box of four crystal glasses, unopened package of men's t-shirts. A beach towel. The delightful things pin me to sorrow. *That bird.*

How to mourn someone who has not died? Although I know when a parent dies, the relationship still continues.

flocks

John says—about the lover's own ambivalence—*if the relationship isn't conflicted then you should worry.* What would I do without *him*?

*

One morning my lover calls from a hotel bed one hundred miles away to say, *sometimes I feel complete relief having left her.* Or did he say, *grief*?

*

I thought during my husband's long 10 p.m. walks that maybe he was purchasing sex in doorways then returning to refuse me. Or just sitting on the median strip, hanging out with hookers then returning home to his own reticence.

When I finally told him I'm leaving, he curled up in bed and heaved without noise. I grabbed the children and their jackets and pulled them into spring snow—to protect them from his grief? To protect myself? To keep them from both? To keep them to myself?

Is memory the same as recollection? As golden dancing slippers? As a sparrow's birthday cake?

His nightly walks paralleled my constant running off to one café or another, where I could reside safely for a couple hours. The comfort of hearing the clink of silverware washed in the kitchen, "Walk Away Renée" on Lite FM, someone cute attending the bottomless cup.

*

Cid Corman and Kamaike Susumu translated those Bashō lines: *Moon and Sun are passing figures of countless generations, and years coming or going wanderers too.* And the Dorothy Britton version I used as a crib sheet in college: *The passing days and months are eternal travelers in time. The years that come and go are travelers too.*

Maybe memory is really against travel—as it selects which interior to settle into.

*

> In winter everything blackens,
> the frozen ground turning its cold shoulder.
> In this momentary return of mud
> this or that man can exit
> and the veins thaw
> with the rise in temperature. How lovely
> to anticipate the summer's afternoon shade
> so humid it is difficult to breathe.
> Then become that afternoon, if possible.

*

I make my home again and again: café on Sackett, café on President, on 2nd Avenue waiting for John, on 99th waiting for the girls to finish Japanese dance, on 52nd after breakfast with H, in one hotel or other when traveling.

Or kneeling in front of him by the hall mirror, holding his ass. Or his kneeling in front of me as I look in the hall mirror. Or bending over the edge of the bed. Or perching on the desk, stockings off. Or clothes half on, and half in a pile on the floor.

(Do the stacks of magazines, bills, children's toys, coffee cups—do all these things drive me away even as I collect them to nest? *Yes*.)

*

Were family vacations running away from home? *Yes*.

The mice burrowed in as soon as we closed the apartment door and drove to the ferry. We'd return to find them.

And what about this sublet of mine—neatly tended and straightened each night when I tuck my girls in, saying, *sticks-feathers-string-mud—*

*

(The lover's words so unsettling they could override childbirth and ten anniversaries—so absolute, the words were not from his mouth but an echo, a sounding.)

(Elizabeth Barrett Browning called it *my childhood's faith*.)

*

The more the petals blow off the more
I find not grief but summer.
Loss was before—as if in childhood seasons only.
The winter cradled the seed, a wish
for summer light flushing the colors out.

Replying to others—I forgot my self
but returned with the vernal equinox. Yes?
Yes, cherry, plum—
yes, orchard of the aorta.
The season's ruin, the heart's sigh.

Note to myself: jot down words like *warming* and *warning. Cluster* and *cloister. Cease* and *sees. Seize.*

*

That husband will always be the one who pulled the crowning infants—one daughter and the next. Who could not, as I could not, reflect more than one another's wounds.

Wound. Wind.

Wind.

*

Now time changes during flight—it pauses.

Roget's 3rd edition—*Nonexistence* under *verb*—"Cease to be." And I am startled and look up 2.5: "cease . . . perish, expire, die; vanish, disappearing; . . . fade away or out, fly, dissolve . . . come to nothing." *Yes.*

(Legs straddling a vanity sink to wash before lovemaking. My powder and oils in the lover's medicine cabinet.)

*

Does the wren cry
when it cries into the graying air, confettied with seed?
A boy skips rope
on the pavement pink with torn blossoms. Then what?
Is the dragonfly afraid to love
what it may not understand?
The firefly? The firefly waits for
nightfall. Does he wait for nightfall?
She does. Though the females clustering together
may not wait at all.
Some may not even respond to light—I think.
But that is summer.
Could this be August?

*

Each *he*, first a vehicle for takeoff, then the impulse for the takeoff itself.

Okay.

Are they okay—the Swamp, Savannah, Field, Fox, Grasshopper, Chipping, Song, White-Throated, White-Crowned, Clay-Colored, Lark, American Tree, Brewer's, Lincoln's, Leconte's, House, Vesper—? These *passerines*?

*

But even humidity
is not a cure and warm rain
not a tonic
for bitterness: *look,*
I tell my daughters,

see how a magnifying glass
can light paper in the courtyard.
I linger there by the pink dogwood
now only a rustling green.
Does the stoop matter?

*

I could not return to the body that contained only the literal world.

Where *sparrow* does not suggest *sorrow.*

Where *sorrow* does not suggest *sorry.*

The Narrow Road—scattered tanka, ii.

Boerum Hill, September 2001

Firefighters print their social security numbers on their arms before digging
into the rubble for their comrades. Digging into ash for a pulse.

Where I once sold rep ties to brokers, now the floor is a makeshift morgue
lined with the burnt and shattered. This is as far as I allow my imagination.

Day eleven: after days of sun and two of rain, the soles of the rescue workers'
boots melt on the still-feverish metal wreckage.

*

Conspiring with Shikishi

The evening mist forming in my heart: the one daughter runs off into that
dark. The other watches.

Loneliness is the habit of this apartment—the bowl of flowers that, outside,
would still root in the frost.

Really—who cares about the moon over the skyline—who cares about him—
and who cares about what I thought was my heart—

*

From "Opening Her Text"

Increasingly my daughter strays outside—the heart's curfew brings her back.

The Artist's Daughter

(2002)

One of two favorite quotes is from Louise Glück—"We look
at the world once, in childhood. / The rest is memory." And,
when I recall the workshop I had with her, in my memory,
she'd advise us to "choose." I imagined an x-acto-knife or
razor—both tools that Father used in cutting paper to the
right breath. I mean *breadth*.

On Mondays and Wednesdays I babysat her three-year-old.
I'd slip a package of orange peanut-butter crackers into my
pocket and we'd walk the couple blocks to the train tracks.
Sit and watch the Rock Island Line. Also, when his bear lost
his eyes, I sewed buttons on that fuzzy face.

I recall she wore "green" perfume.

Exhuming a Cento

That extreme behavior—necrophilia—must be a matter of possession—whether consuming, fucking, chopping into manageable parts. Souvenirs.

I wish I could kill off his past. Cut slabs into tiny unidentifiable pieces. That his mentioning of thinking about his former life is a kind of necrophilia.

Arrondissements

Les catacombes

Note: Gein's skull trophies and skinsuits and Dahmer's refrigerator are all indexed under *Wisconsin*.

Repetition comforts. Preserves an ache from childhood as if preserving a question.

Note: "Hellwig reports that a mother in order to cure her hermaphrodite son opened the grave of a virgin. The son had to follow the counsel of the mother and lie naked upon the corpse 'to bring his sex in order.' He was discovered the next day dead in this position."

Freud on burying memories and antiquities: "Their burial had been their preservation." Similarly, Sarah Boxer noted in the *New York Times* that "there's a price for digging up the dead" since the excavation is "the beginning of the demise." She quoted another writer: "the closer you get to [a dead body], the more alluring it is."

Note: Stunning—that words exist for these activities. My favorite is *exhume*.

Details fascinate, fasten. I see their raw events as a private lexicon.

See "The Unquiet Grave," page 76 of *The Norton Anthology of Poetry*, Third Edition.

Gilles des Ray—

(In her bathroom, I was reluctant to try her perfume—especially since the evidence would be obvious. But I noted the French name and tried the spray at a store downtown. I can still feel the pungency in my throat.)

The pediatrician T. Berry Brazelton wrote: "The goal of attachment is detachment."

She mistypes: *Their burial had been her salvation.*

In Childhood

things don't die or remain damaged
but return: stumps grow back hands,
a head reconnects to a neck,
a whole corpse rises blushing and newly elastic.
Later this vision is not True:
the grandmother remains dead
not hibernating in a wolf's belly.
Or the blue parakeet does not return
from the little grave in the fern garden
though one may wake in the morning
thinking mother's call is the bird.
Or maybe the bird is with grandmother
inside light. Or grandmother was the bird
and is now the dog
gnawing on the chair leg.
Where do the gone things go
when the child is old enough
to walk herself to school,
her playmates already
pumping so high the swing hiccups?

Charming Lines

i.

As she twirls around her skirt swirls up.
She lifts her pink flannel skirt.
The black river snakes through the blue forest.
He drops the orange stones on the gray path.
Thank you, moon!
Although every story is about severing cords.
The bread. The furnace. We walk home
with pockets full of frightful gold.

ii.

The house overlooks a bitter garden.
So dark green it is black.
A mother spills milk on the blue tile.
The white rivulet streams out the kitchen door
over everything but the neighbor's alive greens.
Elbows confess to splinters from the windowsill.
The daughter's yellow hair will become a golden ladder.
As she twirls around her skirt swirls up.

iii.

The girl adores her pink dog.
Her mother adores her and her own mother.
As she twirls around her skirt swirls up.
She may not bring her dog to her grandmother
whose fever is hectic.
The long pink path collapses.
The red cloak. The basket. The jagged teeth.
The hot smell as if grandmother left the iron on.

iv.

Her nails are pink and white.
A sunrise is pink and white.
The tree behind the mill bears cherries.
Sometimes the fruit is so familiar
even the jays do not pluck any.
Ah, little girl! Oh, little daughter!
As she twirls around her skirt swirls up.
The crows realize raw stumps.

v.

She ran holding the jar and fell,
cutting open her chest.
The scar does not mar her beauty.
As she twirls around her skirt swirls up.
The bite of apple does not corrupt—
not the crust of sleep in her eyes.
Seven pairs of fingers smudge the glass.
She can think in her dream state that she dreams.

vi.

The caterpillar droppings sound like rain
outside her room behind the kitchen
where the ashes are gray and gentle.
The mice are rats.
The mother is dead.
The real mother is always dead.
As she twirls around her skirt swirls up.
Those rags that smell like foresight.

vii.

The mother had sewn doll dresses from scraps
of her own silk and chiffon hems.
Even the oldest girl prizes her doll.
As they twirl around their skirts swirl up.
The twelve sisters lift their gowns.
The father betrays by being a father; the child, the child.
So, their dancing slippers wear thin each night.
In bed their ecstatic feet pulse with blisters.

The Two Sisters

The older sister is severe and sallow,
while the other is the rosy girl
we learn about before bedtime.
The other is also the faithful one
who bargains with a bilious ogre
to save her parents from the plague
then finds herself covered with scales
until rescued by a man not her father.
She's also the girl the mother delighted carrying
like a narrative—
their mother, *our mother*,
the seventh and final child
of sugarcane plantation hands;
our mother, the daughter who feared
glinting shark fins
spied off the black beaches,
who saved horseshoe crabs
flipped over on the sand,
and who covered her small breasts
when neighbor boys peeked inside the bathhouse
where she sang songs she could not understand—
all this a cousin told us in the still air
of that same rough house.
The younger sister would also be
kept inside like a keepsake.
This was the conclusion.
And my overwhelming punishment
for being firstborn is that I, too,
adore you—sister, loveliness, hearth—
and that there is never room for two.

*

The older sister recalls pressing her ear
to her mother's swollen belly
rolling in thumps
which she knew because she was told
was a tiny baby.
She imagined a knot of flesh nestled in blood.
She wondered if her mother would push it out
like the cat excreting a half dozen kittens.
And if the mother would eat or discard an imperfect one.

*

Perhaps the two sisters really belong inside
the one self—
inside me, the firstborn.
Although even if they do reside
in my own chest
I still send that Oldest figure out
while the Youngest stays
to scour the bathroom porcelain
and tear feathers off a chicken
then boil it. With Mother.
Knead dough, braid then bake
with Mother. The Oldest leaves
because her pulse depends on departing
from the rooms that hold light
like holding one's breath.
She needs to crawl through brambles
on a moonless night. She needs to know
the roots cradle animals with sharp teeth.
The Youngest's lungs work best
inside that collection of rooms
containing tiny circles of light under each lamp

not unlike an aquarium.
In this dark hum
she displays her iridescence,
plays in and out of the poisonous fingers of the anemone.
And the bubbles.
It is the Oldest that likes
her already swelling breasts.
She could leave, not look over her shoulder
at the cottage that vanishes into thin twilight
and not hear anyone call *goodbye* or *come back*—
if anyone calls.
*
Maybe the sisters lost their parents
even before the second daughter could speak.
Maybe the two orphans kept house
under a hundred tree branches
and held each other
so when strangers passed by
they saw only one swollen shadow—
a monstrous girl with two heads
rocking in grief, rocking in safety.

Consumed

Apart from ancient custom there is
some other urgency, as in Gruner's 1771 report on

a Mr. Goldschmidt, a cowherder for twenty-eight years,
and lacking in the extraordinary;

the document presents that after a quarrel with a traveler

who Goldschmidt claimed had frighted his beasts,

he struck him down with a stick.

To avoid detection, he cut the dead man into sections,
smuggled then boiled

then ate each piece at home. At length
discovered eating a child

he had enticed into his kitchen, he admitted
he had cultivated a taste for human flesh.

And in Pyle and Gould's landmark 1896 *Medical Anomalies*

there was a man from Bicêtre, who,
though he did not have the courage to kill,

craved intestines—and so
prowled around graveyards for the putrid meat

of which he would regale himself

before filling his pockets for future feasting.

What of these tastes that try all other impulses?
*
Likewise, Rodericus à Castro in 1617 wrote in
De universa muliebrium morborum medicina

of a pregnant woman who so desired
the doughy shoulder of her local baker

that she killed him then salted his flesh
which she then devoured, piecemeal.

What of those tastes that are finally beyond sacrament?
*
What of an appetite we only dream of if we dream
of the mother or father in a pine box, fleshy arms
laid across a fleshy chest
and silenced heart? Those hearts
kept from the child, finally, for one another—

it's true. What of the parent's appetite
for the child who cannot survive without
offering that proverbial arm and a leg—I am
sorry I kept leaving the childhood home,
packed more into pockets until I'd finally gone

from that house under a million trees,
two million stars and even more screeches
outside the bedrooms in the blackened air.
Leaving behind another meal, a sister.
Leaving with my body and my body's small hunger.
*

Likewise, a woman in 1817
was found cooking the amputated leg of a small child.
*

Likewise, in 1780, Georgius Prochaska reported
in *Adnotationum academicarum*

on a woman in Milan who drew children
into her home to slaughter, salt and consume—

was it to make them stay always?
*

Leaving one or another lover, smuggling home
his leftovers from the bulletproofed Chinese takeout—
what could finally remain but an emptiness to fill
next door to some other fast-food joint?
*

Yet another puzzle lies not
in *the morbid adhesions between the brain*

and the cerebral membranes
discovered by nineteenth-century surgeons—

or in acquired or inherited tastes—
but in the research itself. Who was Pyle or Gould?

Who was this Castro—
and did he spend his days sweating

in the unheated clipping morgue of the Medical Library

or blowing on his cold fingers in the autopsy amphitheater—
did he excuse himself from the dinner table

to jot down a note on the lovely texture
of liver before finally asking, *Why me?*

Like Lavrinia

Like Lavrinia Merli, in 1890 in Majola, Mantua,
expired from hysteria and placed in a vault

on Thursday, July 3, where she regained consciousness,
tore at the grave clothes her peasant husband had just

smoothed around her seven-month pregnant belly,
and where she turned over and gave birth

but was not discovered until Saturday—
both mother and newborn then really dead;

like George Hefdecker of Erie, Pennsylvania,
a farmer, who upon suffering heart failure in 1891,

was temporarily buried until the purchase of a plot
and was unearthed four days later

with his fingers so bitten off his hands no longer looked human;

like Mr. Oppelt, a wealthy manufacturer in Rudenberg
whose vault, unsealed fifteen years after his death,

was found to contain a skeleton
seated in the corner, the coffin lid off;

like the beggar turned up frozen in a German village in 1807 and buried

only to be disinterred when a watchman detected

lamentations from the grave

though by that time he had indeed suffocated;
like them, yes, the air about my body dead

even in this abrupt consciousness.
*
He sips his instant coffee black
and turns on 1010 WINS.

The apartment is in the back of a storefront.

The neighborhood kids piss under the door.
Our bedroom is so drafty

we sleep in layers of sweats
and stuff old towels in window cracks.

But it isn't the boys or the draft

that keeps me from opening my eyes.
Not the traffic update or Dow Jones. Not even

that man setting his cup down on the counter

to whack a mouse with a broom. If
I press my ear to the pillow

I can mistake my pulse for awareness.
It's the light even when the lights are off.
*
He closes the door on the newly hung wallpaper

and the dishes soaking in sudsy gray gravy
for his nightly walk down Broadway

communing with Black hookers and White junkies.
He is looking for oxygen. I am the wife

under the fluorescent bathroom light

tweezing each hair around my sex.

It vaguely hurts. It reminds me that feeling
is not what I will get from him. It kills time

until "Miami Vice." Afterwards
the infant daughter will wake just as we lie down.
*
There are several reported happy endings.
Like the farm wife Mrs. Sarseville,

who, in 1891, while milking cows
saw beneath the floorboards

a nest of snakes and fell to the ground

then presumed dead by her physician and loved ones
until she sat upright in her coffin.

Her daughter led the woman to the breakfast table
where she ate heartily. Ah!

It is amazing they are found ever.

Figures

Less obvious than a Hindoo goddess
Blanche Dumas possessed surplus legs and genitalia

though, so to speak,
everyone really possesses supernumerary parts.

As for Blanche
she could practice coitus in both openings,

in both, realize arousal. Lucky girl—
but what of the wife whose husband did not know

to spread both pairs of legs? who did not persist
in the little apartment with a double-wide bed

—what of that wife who, in seeking her nerve endings

when the husband turned away from her limbs

with their monstrous surplus needs, sought

boundless affection that even numerous boy lovers
could not finally fulfill with their earnest suck—

why couldn't that wife just pause her
stunning need to figure up? Myrtle Corbin

from Texas, double-bodied from the waist down,

gave birth to three children from one vagina, two
from the second. Did one body want

the other to go away, to not attract—or
is that never an issue for the twinned? I cannot

imagine not, as I rise to leave the bedclothes

folded over the husband who otherwise deals go-fish
to one daughter, plays hide-and-seek with the other,

buys them chocolate squares but cannot tell

what to make of the parasitic body dangling
from my pelvis. *Do it,* I could instruct,

Do the monster you married, or I'll leave for good.

Even so, I wonder if I really remained long after
the ceremony of champagne and pastries—?

I apologize for presenting real persons
to illustrate *this wife's* predicament, and yet,

imagine their imagination unconflicted because

when each pees, she pees from two holes at once.

Which is only human. Which even one midwife,
who tossed the supernumerary creature

under the bed and ran out the door,

knew in her adequate heart (this, the sideshow after all).

And will the husband finally notice and say, *Just get lost,*
but leave the door ajar, sensing he too

trails a duplicate appendage—

or lives like Johnny Eck, born with half a body,

which makes one wonder at the photograph
of such a robust chest that is his whole body—

just how he defecated? how
he hopped on the piano bench

in the sea breeze of his parents' summer cottage,

doors closed on the neighboring girls—

how he loved with more than his heart?

I told one boy lounging on a train platform,
the boy I loved, that couples part more often

at this opening of the millennium because
fewer believe in the existence of a heaven—
and why, after confusing lack and excess, should we?

From "The Skin"

Claw out the heart,

decapitate the surprised expression,

skin the still live body

and pull the sleeves of flesh

over your own delirious limbs

so you dance robed

in its nakedness:

Here I am. Here it is.

Here are instructions for an ancient rite.

From Reckless Sonnets

2.

How lavish are the pheromones? How
iridescent the scent that radiates
from the female for the male's
compound eyes that
cannot afford mistaking
stem for leg, leaf for wing?
How stunning is daylight for coupling
even or especially for the praying mantis
whose female devours the male
after that single climax? How
does one turn to sleep
in the same bed once made bloody
first with love then with love—
and how does one stay
seated in the kitchen listening to the percolator
after that knowledge?

3.

The wingspan six-feet-wide a million years ago,
the dragonfly is now the iridescent whir
over meadow and pond—the pond where
the offspring nymphs hatch and crouch
among murky reeds and roots
to snatch at any wriggling thing.
After two years underwater, the adolescent
attaches to a stem and climbs out of its skin
looking forward to two sets of lucid wings.

How to imagine an airborne insect
that starts its life completely aquatic? How
to imagine several sets of skin translucent and tense
and finally as easy to discard as,
if not a first lover, the second or third?

11.

For two millennia, the instars have been the stars—
treasured by farmers who, for a pound of silk, gather
twenty-five thousand cocoons, drop them in hot water
to kill the chrysalid and soften the gummy threads.
Less known, the silkworm moth has no mouth
so cannot eat in its three-day existence
laying four hundred eggs in mulberry leaves.
I flare open a sheet woven from caterpillar spit
for a lover. For saliva, blood, and cum.
For two to three days of anonymous flight. For
the sensation that this coupling will last a hundred years,
that it will end after a moment, wing-torn and starved.

Daphne's Words

i.

Pulling the cord back you can feel
your own tendon a part
of the arrow's Attention
trained on a wing. This
is where I live—on the spongy moss,
in the brambles that catch in hair—
where you can taste the ozone
before a storm—hear the first drops
on the canopy before the downpour. If
I cross the laconic Threshold
to the vestibule of suitors
I risk reducing the heart to a trophy
and atrophy—
or risk returning the gut to an exile
one learned in those first steps away from mother
when the mother saw you turn
and quickly left to save her self.
I cannot recall a woman's Affection
after that lesson in walking
but live on the belief
she loved me as much as the Earth
adores Tubers.

ii.

The mother had to leave—yes?
so there was no longer a kiss against
the tree's shadows
through the cracked window
now closed lest the daughter
follow—look for the mother
to seek Care and Fault. If
she is hawking woven mats
in the dust of the marketplace
I will find her and ask *why?*
And She will recall
I was born feet first—
that she loved me though the midwife
warned there would be few congratulations—
adored Me even before
she glimpsed my eyes
tearing from the sudden light
and squinting her face into Focus.

iii.

Hearing my scream—
my father bound me by his own
ambiguous bank—
root in clay, branch
trawling currents.
How I wish to uproot
and hunt again the Woods
I knew before men

determined my predicament
but not my fate. Always
I have thrown my self
into the River I call father.

iv.

Mother, when you returned
you only recognized me by my Scent, laurel—
an allusion
induced by your husband, my father. Why
return now that my aureola have budded,
my labia unfolded? After
I've already run into trouble?
Come to see if I still have
your eyes? how petulant
even this Female is? Come to check
how miserably this girl turned out after all—
here where a man-raised daughter
is convented to punish men?
Do you return to these god-infested woods
to root me out?
If I had hands
I would still ask to comb your Hair.

v.

There's something to be said for Mud—
I will say one day
as I recall the smell of silt, sand, pebbles,
and the chill of wet clay

red as newborn red.
This is the Dream of the laurel's finite twigs:
that one day I will say, *Father, I leave. Goodbye—*
a departure once disallowed
a daughter with no Tongue;
that one day this Recollection will tease
my own daughter's urgent Ears.

The Dark Light

I sit looking at the white paper graying on my desk
and recall being an adolescent
in the same light: not
being able to move into the world
that wants you to do everything
the way it wants. The backstroke.
Touch-typing.
Cutting a dress from a pattern.
An A-line. Cotton.
A pink daisy print
spread smooth on the Home Ec. table,
pins between my lips.
Later hemmed at home. This was when
we had to wear dresses to school.
This was when I knew I'd marry one day
but first have an office of my own.
This office is light, or dark really,
the way my room was always dark
so I could avoid being the daughter
in the rooms with lamps.
How I wish you would turn your car
away from your wife and daughters
and return to this square of dark light
so familiar, as I've already said,
it fails to pulse with grief.

Mosquito and Ant

(1999)

When I ran a reading series in the Chatham Public Library, I invited Trinh Minh-ha to read. What a rewarding way to curate—inviting the author of a work that was becoming part of my body—

Speaking, writing, and discoursing are not mere acts of communication; they are above all acts of compulsion. Please follow me. Trust me, for deep feeling and understanding require total commitment.
  Woman, Native, Other

This was around the time I was drawn to the phrase *writing the body* but had difficulty finding examples. For years. Finally, after falling in love with Bishop—which I wasn't at first—I came to see how she engendered the body in her poetry. The vertiginous experience that can arrive with a frightening realization: The waiting room "was sliding / beneath a big black wave, another, and another." Yes. And, the alliteration in such a short line is as experiential as the literal meaning.

More than ever—I wish to draw the body back in.

I wish for a drawer of spondees.

Mosquito and Ant, a cento

"Why do you interrupt whenever I'm reading?" he asked the night before.

She feels buried: that there is no feeling left in her body, only the idea of feeling.

She is running late.

When had his heart become that heart / withdrawing from the whorls of her offerings?

She leashes the dog and, as she steps out the door, forgets the keys.

A list of categories by her translator:
> *Things that make one's heart beat faster*
> *Things that arouse a fond memory of the past*
> *Oxen should have very small foreheads*
> *A preacher ought to be goodlooking*
> *It is so stiflingly hot*

At the corner pay phone / the heart throbs publicly.

Her name?

Imagine words with a dimension / not unlike the light and dark regions / of the moon. The back of planets. The craters. / Words that orbit the body / like a plea granted.

Save clipping: / "Secret Life of Jupiter's Moons."

We do not know her name.

The scent like a pleased cry.

If she touches herself, she can / find that pulse that sounds like an echo.

She loves her own voice radiating off the tiles.

Every time she speaks it is a leave-taking.

Perhaps you know her name!

Perhaps there are a certain number of souls that circulate. Perhaps Mother is an infant, now learning to speak. To touch a mirror. A child with her own mother.

Perhaps she became the mother / she thought she had had.

Wax

initial correspondence to Elle—

i.

I am looking for clues
on how to stay a woman, not
a middle-aged woman
who sings all those girl-group lyrics
over the dash
but a woman since
I've earned that title
over the years of (honey, you know—)
wicked repartees
among my girlfriends and boyfriends.
Here's the subtext:
the twenty-year-olds
at poetry readings
are so exquisite they might be
fashioned of wax, even
the blemishes. I realize now
how lithe I was when I thought
I was the ugly daughter—how
tremulous my beauty. I didn't know.
I just knew
I wanted to fuck my professor
(Chaucer 8:30 am M/W)
and boys from Chinese History
wearing blue caps. Nixon
was still President.
The war was nearly over.
And the young now listen
to fifty-year-old rockers.

No wonder they don't think
they invented sex. Fuckin-A
we did.
And what I want at some moment
in my forties
is not an affair—
that would rip my breast open—
I would like to wrap my arms around a guy
(I guess a guy)
for a lengthy kiss.
Standing up. In the dark.
Pulse at the boiling point
one recalls
from those irretrievable initial encounters.
Dear one—send me advice quick.

ii.

waxing

iii.

I send these words to you
across the frozen continent,
through waning light
and steam rising off rivers.

Kafka's Erection

i.

Elle, my lovely older sister,
I suggest to *you* what to say
to a former lover?
With two children my own longing often
feels alien—
the breast for nursing, the genitals
for birth (forget conception—).
As one daughter loses her teeth, the other
increasingly pierces her body
and both learn to say *fuck you* in the school yard.
And I am more *the older woman* each day.
As for *your* lover—well
after he sits at the table for lunch, I'd
loop around him to pour water
and lean close to his face—
so close there is barely air between.
Then see what happens.

ii.

My husband wants to know why
I carry your poems around with me.
As if a cashmere scarf. Or air tank.

iii.

In infancy we travel from *mama* to *no*.
Then? A roundtrip?

iv.

I scribbled a ten-page letter to you months ago.
It is folded on my nightstand among bills and bracelets.
And Kafka.

v.

I imagine us swimming to a sand bar.

vi.

Tell me what you'd do
with seven black slips
purchased at thrift shops.
I mean to wear them as dresses.

Mosquito and Ant

i.

The Immortal Sisters:
One has only daughters.
One has a husband and a lover.
One has two ex-husbands.
One has a rock band.
One doesn't give a shit.
One has a lover fourteen years younger.
One is losing her lover.
One is losing her lover to breast cancer.
One writes on her coffee breaks at a bilingual program.
One circles an island in her station wagon.
One's first son just shot himself.
One wants a donor egg.
One tattoos fireflies on her back.
One can't speak to the others.
One searches for the others as her source of immortality.
Another—immorality.

ii.

At the café with pink marble tables
I imagine you still asleep, a profile
across the continent that darkens
from this ocean to your own.
On separate coasts, the seals turn and twist.
In lakes, fish pierce the surface for nymphs.
Perhaps you stayed up late
rereading *reptiles of the mind*
or *moths of consciousness*. Perhaps

you drafted a letter.
I'm trying to write
while a child repeatedly asks
if bleeding hurts.
Your oldest daughter
asks what her name means
and perhaps you think of
a day you asked your mother the same.
My mother is dead
and yours is living.
You tell me:
She still cooks for herself.
Or was that my mother?
This correspondence blossoms like sea anemone
ingesting the krill of our hearts.

iii.

She
Shi in Japanese: four, poem, death.

In Chinese?
In *mosquito and ant* script?

(*Yes*, in Chinese, yes.)

iv.

I want my letters to resemble
tiny ants scrawled across this page.
They spy a crumb of dark sugar

on the far side of the embankment
and their strategy is simple:
the shortest distance between two points
is seduction not tenacity.

I want my letters to imitate
mosquitoes as they loop
around the earlobe with their noise—
Those spiderlike legs. The sheaths of wings.
There's the impossible task of slapping one
across its erratically slow travel.
That body that transports disease.
(I wonder if a straight man can decrypt such lines.)

I want my letters to resemble the smoke
when the widower burned his young wife's poems
so she might polish them in heaven.
The smoke not unlike that from burnt toast or punk.

I want my forbidden script to be bidden.

Jam

i.

He tells me I better not
be fooling around
as I lick cappuccino froth
off a plastic lid. He tells me
he knows what's up
then wonders out loud
if a friend is
screwing around.
I tell him she
may be manipulative
but not so devious as to
complain she's not getting any
while she's getting some
on the side. I am
that devious
but if I were I wouldn't
be telling him. He
grins and says
yeah right. Tosses his cup
into the trash
and puts his hand
on the small of my back. He says
he knows
what's going on. Which, I say,
is nothing as long as you're supplying
the jam.

ii.

He tells me not to drink alone
and I tell him, I'm not. I'm writing
to her. He tells me
the same the next evening as he turns on
the News. I miss my self.
Dear Elle, you tell me I count on him
to retrieve my own body.

iii.

jam, jelly, preserves,—

iv.

He turns on the 7 o'clock news. He
reads the Final Edition. He turns on
the 11 o'clock news. He reads
a spy thriller. He turns in.

v.

I tell him, Remember how
the wind blew spray
off the crests of waves? How
some nights our footprints
were phosphorescent?
And he says, What?

vi.

Meanwhile I read how female adepts
found students. I read how many
considered these women as *travelers*
from another dimension. I read
these chapters on the Immortal Sisters
and my fingertips tingle
as if catching breath.
My blood quickens as if to rip tide.

The Tumbler

i.

I call you.
I pour one then while on the phone
pour more
rye over a tumbler of ice.
I call you
to hear your voice:
if you've received the poems,
to tell you sorry I lost your article.
To hear you ask if
I am giving to others
the tendrils I should be giving myself.
I call to hear you
tell me you love me
though you say so to everyone.
There.

ii.

You think wisteria
is a vine
that climbs suitable trees
in suburban gardens
and gridded parks:
then down the street you see a whole tree
with the fruitlike blossoms.
Can you guess what I'm saying?

iii.

You say you are curious
about what my new poems are "about."
I write this:
I've hardly eaten
for a week
and realize I need the hunger pangs
to match the longing for some thing—maybe
to sleep in your basement again,
maybe for that kid lingering on the corner,
cigarette hanging from the pouting lip.
Most likely the nicotine itself
from the second-hand smoke.

iv.

X sends a card—
he writes he cannot sleep because I am
on his mind.
And I imagine when he does fall out
I am just rising and pulling a slip over my shoulders.
I can almost hear the ivy clinging to the stucco.

v.

You think the morning glories open
because you open
in that light
where we both see so clearly
a coat tree, a box of old magazines,
a child's pull-toy caterpillar.
And they do.

vi.

You think I am ripped open
to the moon's movements.
And you are right.

Garnet

i.

X wanted to present a gift
the husband would not detect
as inclination. Book bag.
Rhyming dictionary. Hand mirror.
I copied poems from *The Orchid Boat* for him.

ii.

You are the Empress Wu Tsu-T'ien
requesting her lover
examine her *pomegranate dress.*
I am as delighted as you.

iii.

Eating a bowl of raspberries
I imagine X sucking
on the beads on my garnet necklace—

iv.

She began as concubine to Emperor T'ai then to his son, Emperor Kai, until
he replaced his Empress with her. She ruled China from that moment. After
his death and into old age, she kept a male harem, concubines and courtier
lovers. How do you feel about that?

v.

nipples the color of garnet

vi.

You advise, why dull a sharp point?
why flatten the crests? why
rinse out color? why douse what
the gut claims from the heart—

vii.

the *he* residing in the *she*

viii.

garnet hard as nipples—

Orchid Root

i.

Who thinks of the orchid root
but the horticulturalist
or the one now holding shears
and a jar of water.
Who thinks of soil
but the gardener when
even the scent of mulch completes the air
like light.

ii.

my hands smell like tobacco
from his shirt that smells of my hand cream

iii.

I need to return to the Chinese women poets.
The tones of pine and orchid.
The clouds playing over the crescent moon.
Return to the coy lines
that protest and advertise.
The words weighted in
object and objection
as much as flight.
If there was a bridge outside my window
I would slip on silk slippers
the ones with a phoenix
and run across

to the sisters who know
how to instruct the senses:
when to know the difference
between the narcissus's fragrance
and burning rubber.

iv.

Take the anonymous courtesan
who wrote the lines:
My hairpins on your fallen jacket—
My stockings on the tiles—
My petals on your root—

v.

The women write poems to one another
to protest the man's inattention:
and they fall in love
consequently
as honeysuckle climbs the fence
from one garden to the next
its fragrance on the draft beneath the door.

vi.

PINE   松

MAGPIE   鵲

CLOUD   雲

vii.

C can read classical Chinese
and I envy her like the bitch
I was born to be:
haughty *and* self-effacing.
Always wanting.
Always evasive.
What saves me is my knowing
if I don't want to write about something
there is nothing else to write.
This is what compels me
to locate the characters in *Matthew's*.

viii.

the grass radicals—

ix.

Clearly, I need the taste of plum
on my hands, my chin, his lips.
His. Mine. Plumb.

Clippings

the mundane in between correspondence

i.

What I learned on this past trip:

Sexual tension is never disappointing.

There are black stingrays with white polka dots.

Coral is a type of anemone.

(Some somersault. Some move at a rate of four inches/hour.)

Lower one's expectations in men.

Some sexualize activities, some sublimate sexual energy.

Speed camera on Utopia Pkwy, driving south.

Marxism is not dead.

The point of life is stimulation, whether photosynthesis or ballet.

A can lead to B then become B.

ii.

Note to self:

Forgot to mention in my last letter

how a friend's bird

is in love with a paper towel tube.

It fluffs its crown and wings,

struts of course,

then rubs its brow and

attempts to push its head into the tube.

iii.

What I noticed on this past trip:

when I am away from you, I feel homesick—

that feeling of nausea and hunger,

full and partial. Bleeding and bled.
Of missing a part of the body—
have you seen it?

iv.

Save clipping:
The cuscuta in Bryant Park
strangles then sucks
the ivy in the northwest corner.
Also known as *devil's guts*
and *lady's laces,*
if the parasite sprout
does not find a host immediately
it creeps along,
the tip growing, the rear dying off,
till it finds something
to coil around.
Horticulturalists
advise gardeners to weed by hand
or spray MCPA or DCPA.

v.

Save clipping:
"Secret Life of Jupiter's Moons."
Their molten cores may allow
enough change
for life. We can see the cracks
on the bald surface
through the delighted telescope.

vi.

What I noticed this past hour—
the spirit nestles in the mundane
not the fantastic. So
I look in my bowl of cereal.
A basin of suds.
A tank of clown fish.

Radiator

i.

Any strong sensation is a welcome break
from oxygen—

ii.

horse manure outside the stable
cigar smoke saturating the train seats
steamed asparagus from the steamer

iii.

I am not sure what I want
except that he wants
much the same: coal, flint, radiator.
But is X more
of my heart than my heart?

iv.

Any sensation penetrates my skin.
The cold porcelain tub,
the splintered deck,—

v.

X could last into the first snowfall,
the predicted blizzard.
And no, you don't, I think to tell him,
wish I were your girlfriend.

vi.

For the taste of his mouth:
the acid of coffee and tobacco, the acid
of initial encounter—

vii.

Elle—please advise—
what thread can stitch the flesh
back into one piece—

Chuang Tzu's Mistress Sleeps in a Draft

She dreams she leans over the brown dust
and lifts a brown leaf that is a moth,
holds it inside her mouth
to revive the flutter from a frost
now covering the still-live grass,
the fallen pears half eaten by deer,
and her shoulders suddenly exposed
from the comforter
her lover always drags to his side of the mattress
as he turns away in sleep.
Or was it a monarch? she mutters.

Notes from "Nitro"—

I love how multiple meanings for one word can give way to a bit of unconscious material.

Words can be as unstable as nitroglycerin.

Such changeability can make for productive ambiguity: a simple word becomes a portal out of denotation *and* out of logical sense. Such usage resists easy context and linear thinking.

Ambiguity is even more crucial in Japanese poetics. In a haiku, one word can explode the narrow seventeen syllables.

And from "A Dusting," the *vacuum* in the line "The mother lived in a vacuum" must convey the literal vacuum cleaner as well as a space devoid of matter.

Every few years I reread Earl Miner's *Introduction to Japanese Court Poetry* to review *kakekotoba, honkadori, makurakotoba*, and so on.

These terms have led me to find favorite words: *pine, rose, leaves, hedges*. Also, *alarm, vanity, threshold*.

Envelopes of innuendo—

Responding to Light

i. Every desire has a relation to madness . . .
—Luce Irigaray

In the house with windows that look out
into the branches of a forest, into
the dinner of sunsets,
no one is permitted to speak
over the five o'clock news and no one
can see the television but the father.
Here the daughters chew the meal
that will keep them larger than desired,
than desire itself. Here
the father's paycheck purchases the meat
the mother stews.
Here the silent daughters are silenced
like the undergrowth across the street.

In the house with the father's still lifes
of massive seashells and slippery marine life
the daughters imagine the canvases are windows
without blinds. When the two
leave for school on the road by the elms
the younger one asks about the gnarled branches
that grow away from air toward the water table.

And once a year the girls share small, foiled hearts:
the taste of chocolate stimulating and simulating
what cannot be said though there are noises.

ii. . . . our society and our culture operate on the basis of an original matricide.

Somewhere in the small house with no hallways
the mother disappeared
just before the oldest daughter's plump body
too early sprouted hair
and too early, though any time was too early,
budded nipples. This daughter already
knew since third grade that she would bleed
and in the telling had shivered uncontrollably
as if there was no such thing as a radiator.
(If *I* had told her that early evening
I would have held her
and not let go. I would not have left the room.)
And when the girl did bleed
in her baggy cotton underpants
she stuffed them with tissue
then later hid them between the wall and mattress.

SOAR
SORE
SOEUR
SOUR
SUR
SURE

The curtains were gauzy
because the street and neighbors were far
from viewing inside
the interior of the house that resembled
a heart without blood. Veins without color.

iii. . . . the threatening womb. Threatening because it is silent, perhaps?

The womb says things like
come here go away
or *go away come here,*
darling.

iv. . . . corps-à-corps

They peeled carrots.
They added and divided.
They swapped blouses.
They were more daughters than sisters.
They trimmed each other's hair and pierced their faces.

v. . . . sentences that translate the bond between our body, her body,
the body of our daughter.

If she touches her body in the gray bathroom
the gray light lighting the small window,
squeezes her nipple or flicks her vulva—
if she tastes her taste
she is tasting her mother and daughter.
On the Pacific shoreline the marine life crawls back

from the tidal pool or gives up
the desire to breathe underwater ever again.
If she touches herself, she can
find that pulse that penetrates like an echo.
All this without sounds in the gray light off the green tiles.
All this like the real waves on any shoreline. Even lakes.

vi. We barely . . . have access to fiction!

The stories, even when told by father,
were mother's: the one about the shark
beyond the coral reef,
the poi in kindergarten, the red seaweed
washed onto the beach and collected for dinner—
these were her stories we listened to
in our own heads in the house
with rooms filled with the shadows of limbs.
And she never thought they were *of value.*
She knew though we knew she didn't know
how the words would become not only our stories
but the granddaughters' tales to tell classmates
in the school yard filled with balls and ropes.

Further, every time the daughter *sees* someone
she moves away from the rooms
that imitate the ventricles that are finally only tissue.
Every time she speaks it is a leave-taking
from the sealed-off room she knew existed all along—
toward a stew fragrant with fiction.

Volatile
(1999)

For years I tried writing my own version of "Twenty-One Love Poems" but came up with weak results. Still, every attempt brought me closer to Adrienne. I followed her from the time I read about diving into *the wreck*. In those days, there were not as many poems that offered and modeled a vision of equality.

Today, I am not sure I'd use this quote for an epigraph: *What kind of beast would turn its life into words?* The line made sense for my life then. (When it came to that sequence, what struck me most was her description of a prisoner who had been tortured. I would not have used that quote. It was so much about her context, the poem's context.) Which quote then? I open to the poem and find another favorite line ("Your silence today is a pond where drowned things live . . .") but I don't think it could be claimed by one who has not known the challenges she faced.

Whenever we met, she was considerate. Even kind. And she complimented me on my poem "Seizure." (Could I have written such a poem without such a woman?)

Without a jar of voltas—

A *Volatile* Cento

He pushed her back, lifted the hem over her hips, / kissed her clit until she
begged him, yes, to fuck her—please. / He did. Nicaragua, the pool furniture,
the peacocks, / receded into the Big Dipper the way scenery spins away
/ after you twirl around and round. / They couldn't stand. They couldn't
stand it.

She couldn't stand it. She laughed, "I think I'm a communist!" / And he
answered, "Bueno!" and thought, "Sexy this silly *gringa*."

She hadn't yet read *Dialectical Historical Materialism* / but already had a gut
reaction to *dictatorship of the proletariat* / and *forces of production*

epidemic of overproduction

She hadn't yet been exposed to *the cost of production of a workman is
restricted to the means of subsistence that he requires for his maintenance, and
for the propagation of his race.*

At that moment in Managua, in a former Somoza playground, / she only
knew Capitalism wasn't working / what with its glut of apartments *and*
homelessness or / the dumping of milk *and* hunger.

She did know that, back home, they could not house the strong young
unemployed except in rooms with 1200 beds.

She had heard a union organizer: "It was a slate fall that killed my daddy and
uncle. Miners never die of natural causes."

She did know that, back home, language was undermined by the landscape; /
and the landscape, undermined by *driftmouth, curtain, face, / vein, mantrip,
man—*

She sensed a consonance in rising to seize state power and the humid air
of arousal.

She fastened to a translator because translation sets thought / to the field of
images, the mind's viewfinder, automatic focus. *Claro.*

She was a romantic. Yes. But knew she needed to touch a volcano, / smell the
sulfur to believe. / Contradiction would be the heartbeat of their travels.

(She would, someday, write a twelve-page poem about these travels. Call it
The Volcano's Desire.)

It was in Nicaragua, too, where she recalled the blue and pink stars Mother
stitched / on Tomie and her slips; that in Maui / she saw grandmother
had sewn the same / when she handed her twists of wash in the starched
sunlight. / The stars distinguished each daughter's clothing.

And one sunflower / was so tall he tied it to the fence for support.

Possession
a zuihitsu

that Mother sat beside Yoko and spoke to her before any of us knew about
her death, told her to take care of Father, *go, take care of him,* who was
in critical condition but also did not know about this death that only the
detectives and paramedics knew, strangers who would transfer news not
new to them

that when Yoko dances her face becomes the face of her teacher from
childhood, so to view her is to see someone who moments earlier was
the student

that as a toddler she would situate herself in the backyard and *know* where
to dig up porcelain doll parts, a glass medicine bottle, a rusted bracelet with
the initial *C*—in her private archeology—

that the father painted Adam and Eve with Adam's face turned away as his
own father turned away from him

that I write without thinking
*
Mine.

No, mine.
*
you get your fuckinghands off him girl or you wont have hands for shit
*
"In the end, the [warehouse club] industry's acknowledged low-cost
operator uses its size and market clout to bleed rivals dry." *WSJ,* 11/18/93
*

"Retail consultant Peter Monash estimates that Sam's Club cannibalizes itself in 45% of its markets in quest of a dominant market share." *WSJ*, 11/18/93

*

"[The] idea of using so much cash to suppress [voter] turnout, rather than to increase it, struck many as something new, and odd." *WSJ*, 11/18/93

*

that when he tests a pen he always and unconsciously writes, *but Mom—*

*

that when the five-year-old tantrums she alters her demand as the parent yields: *chocolate milk, too white, not this cup, not this spoon*

*

cleave to the soul

*

that when something else is in control of the body—organs, gesture, voice

*

There is a vast difference between private and personal property—one which the bourgeoisie has blurred to antagonize and terrorize the working class. At issue: who owns the means of production, including one's labor.

*

His son died over ten years ago and only now has he resumed consciously writing about the death as surely as grief transforms into something else. *A rocking chair*

*

turpentine, sesame bath oil, turkey soup—

*

The critic wants her to write identifiably revolutionary (*quote unquote*) poetry so he can critique it in terms of his sectarian past rather than explore future possibilities.

*

"The strangest thing was that her robes were permeated with the scent of the poppy seeds burned at exorcisms. She changed clothes repeatedly and even washed her hair, but the odor persisted." *The Tale of Genji* (Seidensticker translation)

*

"It was as though she were a stranger to herself."
The Tale of Genji (Waley translation)

*

the dispossessed

*

I saw a red bucket then I saw a red car then I saw a fire hydrant then I saw bricks then I saw a stop sign—and the elephant I lost was red and we'll never find it

*

psychosomatic blindness

*

Whether he traveled or stayed home, he could not cease thinking about his deceased wife.

The Glass Bracelets

I know I can only speak for myself
but after reading a simple story in *The News*
I wish I could speak for a ninety-four-year-old woman
who on a day of the full moon of Magha in 1907,
at age seven, was led by her parents
to the Saundatti Temple in Karnataka
and given to the Hindu goddess Yellamma:
the childish glass arm bangles broken,
a nuptial necklace given her—
wedded to the deity Dev, Murali must never
marry a mortal, has never washed or cut
her long stiff mat of gray hair—
her duty was forever to be fucked
by those who came to the Temple.
The Temple where, at onset of menstruation
the child was, and still is, auctioned for the privilege
of tearing her hymen often by
one with syphilis or gonorrhea—
virgins believed to be a certain cure.
It is difficult for me to like men at times,
any man, when such atrocities are sanctioned
by the religious. Atrocities for male pleasure.
And I doubt a woman concocted
the legend of this goddess. And I am fucking mad
and want my daughters
to never leave our small Brooklyn apartment
though I know any room can be the residence
of the secreted—like that of the man in Ocala, Florida,
infecting six of his fourteen children
with venereal disease, fathering his daughter's babies,
beating their faces, beating their faces. This

while the religious target abortion clinics
and rude art. Who
can believe in a god in such a world
when god is made by man for men—
I will not respect a moment of silence
in my children's public school for the sake
of semi-automatic politicians wishing to purchase votes
with their small public piety and
blaring prayers. And if you think this is not a poem
because I've ranted without benefit of a metaphor
think again: the story of Murali
is the story of any infant female or male until
the varicose veins that are the status quo,
that are the "religiously correct,"
are slit and drawn. Until then
you, reader, are the five-year-old boy,
genitals severed and flesh neatly
folded back into a tiny cunt, or
the ten-year-old girl with second-stage syphilis
now lodged in her central nervous system.
Hear me: I will not pray. I will not.

Blindsided

They were always looking for some reason to kill us.

The results of the *always looking* became the women's psychosomatic blindness. How to comprehend this state?

The house was warm and quiet. I needed Mother's permission to walk in the woods. I stood beside her as she washed dishes, as she gazed into the gray suds. "Mom, can you hear me?" I kept asking.

There is a high incidence of women turning what I will call *mad* in Asian American writings: John Okada's *No-No Boy*, Milton Murayama's *All I Asking for Is My Body*, Maxine Hong Kingston's *The Woman Warrior*, Hisaye Yamamoto's *Seventeen Syllables*, Bharati Mukherjee's *Wife*, Wendy Law-Yone's *The Coffin Tree*.

Regardless of point of origin, date of arrival, age, etc. Not everyone is first generation. There is also Fae Ng's *Bone*, the sister's suicide driving the narrative.

They were always looking for some reason to kill us.

My village had become a prison farm.

*

Of 170,000 Cambodian refugees living in the United States, half reside in Los Angeles. Local ophthalmologists noticed a high incidence of vision problems among those women who arrived in the 1980s fleeing Pol Pot's Khmer Rouge. Approximately 150 have lost all or most of their sight though there is nothing physically wrong with their eyes.

The Khmer Rouge took Chhean Im's brother and sister away. They killed her father and another brother *before her eyes*.

During the day they would take people into a big meeting hall and beat them and beat them and we all sat in a circle and were made to watch.

I am surprised they speak to an interviewer. Or perhaps a relative told their story to the doctor who told the interviewer.

From his name I assume the writer is a white male although he could be black or adopted or mixed. Like Winnifred Eaton.

There is nothing wrong with their eyes. I am amazed the body can do this.

"Mom? Mommy—"
*
There was a draft. There was a draft from the crack in the window. I knew the source because I could see the curtain moving.

When the Vietnamese Army tried to liberate her village, the Khmer Rouge began massacring everybody in sight.

Perhaps there were men who lost their vision, but it is unlikely any will ever be found since eighty percent of those killed were male.

These images consume me like a flame. My skin feels scorched, prickly, raw and nauseous.

For the next two years the Khmer Rouge direct Lor Poy to dig children's graves.
*

On learning of my work, he tells me when nuns interviewed Koreans in Hiroshima after the bomb, the survivors *drew a blank*. When inadvertently questioned in Japanese, one began to wail and recall the horrors. Others could also remember the events only in Japanese—not in their mother tongue.

I was standing right beside her, and she couldn't hear me. "Mother?" I repeated.

The body protects the spirit just as the spirit protects the body.

I was standing beside him, and he couldn't hear me. "Did you hear me?" I kept repeating.

*

In prison camp, the Khmer Rouge distributed so little food that her husband and daughter starved. She watched her child starve.

Watched her neighbor get clubbed to death. Watched as others disappeared.

—so the mind reacts to what the body perceives—

"Dissociation," a state of altered consciousness. If I am on a freeway daydreaming and drive past the exit . . . If I . . . Then if I . . .

In 1919, Freud called this physical sacrifice *conversion disorder*. "In this context, the word *conversion* refers to replacing a somatic symptom with a repressed idea."

I continue reading that common symptoms include *blindness, partial or total paralysis, inability to speak, deafness, numbness, difficulty swallowing, incontinence, balance problems, seizures, tremors, and difficulty walking* (Wikipedia)

(She typed *sacriface*.)

*

"Seventeen Syllables" begins in the present, as if in the middle of an argument.

What was reality for these women—how did the images affect their travel from country to country—how did the diaspora affect the images?—

I try to view the phenomena in more than polarities, more than blind but not blind.

The metaphor is not blindness. Not vision. Not hysteria. So, then what? He knew a woman who brought a psychosomatic pregnancy to term. She gave birth. Then what? Psychosomatic nursing? Infanticide?

Does metaphor have anything to do with this blindness—or all to do with it—

*

What of the Thai children—female and male, daily prostituted, vagina and anus torn, bloody, swollen, feverish, bruised, lacerated with disease—who blame themselves for being sold? What of the men who permit themselves to brutalize these brown children?

Are the children's faces still lustrous as my daughters'? Will they permit themselves to feel? We read about them as though this only happens to Thai children or only in Thailand.

Can you hear me?

The child prostitutes, rescued by a group of nuns, were telling their life stories for the first time. Mary, though sold by parents, felt she and the other children must have been bad. It is not only in Thailand.

The virgins were naturally the most expensive. Their price quickly diminished. Considered less prone to AIDS by johns, in fact their young bodies tear easily; the wound, an open invitation to disease.

She told a friend, *I was there and not there. He was pounding my body but I was not there. My body was trying to protect me.*

dis/ease, dis/favor, dis/member, dis/possess, dis/rupt

Rape boys and girls. Sodomize neighbors. Club them. Skin them.
*
I don't want to see this.

I don't want to see this.

I won't see it.

I do not see it.

I do not see.

The prisoners had nothing to eat except snakes, rats, worms, and the dead.

—*conversion disorder*—

—*terms*—

I do not.

I do.
*

At first a number of social workers thought the women were attempting to con the state for public assistance. But they behaved as the blind behave, relying on sound, air movement, a sense of *what a room is like*.

—the diaspora of sight—

Ophthalmologists say their machines register sight, measure brainwave activity picked up through sensors attached to the patient's head.

One of the Angka lifted an infant by the head and beat him to death against a tamarind tree.

Four of the Angka picked up [a man who had perhaps stolen a bit of rice, picked him up] by the arms and legs and threw him alive onto a big fire. After that [lesson] we all went back to work.

—hysterical blindness—

—hysterical bind-ness—
*

In "Seventeen Syllables" the three visit a family whose mother has gone mad. And, in the end, the protagonist's father in a jealous rage takes away her mother's only pleasure, writing haiku. Apart from revealing her past to her daughter, she is completely isolated. She can speak but she will not speak.

In "The Legend of Miss Sasagawara," the woman rarely speaks to the other incarcerated. When she finally speaks, she is seen as "normal." Later in life, after the war, she is finally hospitalized and writes a long poem that refers to an authority figure who betrayed her with, ironically, his moral preoccupations. Her father, the Buddhist reverend?

In one instance terror results in a person's immigration. In another, with blooming expectation, the immigrant arrives but experiences abuse from inside and outside the home. In *The Woman Warrior*, the mother's sister immigrates to reunite with her husband. On finding he has begun a new family she goes mad—hears people who are coming to harm her.

Garbage ghost, mailman ghost, . . . as if turning the real less real? More, rendering them differently real; then marginalizing the inhabitants for a more central existence?

*

Do the women remember more with the visual exile—as if replaying a film in a darkened theater? or do they not see *anything*?

If a person cannot see, what do they see? Black? Gray?

When I shut my eyes, I am exiled into my memories and imagination. I can only leave by admitting sight.

"See? See what I mean?"

When the interview is over, she turns toward the draft whistling in beneath the door.

She didn't know I was standing beside her as she scrubbed dishes. Scoured pans. Even with the water turned off. Her eyes were blank.

These Current Events

It is a late twentieth-century cliché
that we must turn off the hypersensitive television
that distracts our truer desire; that we must
switch off all the lamps and overheads,
open the shade to the natural night
with its artificial lights, dress in silk to undress,
play and play until even the nerve endings in our teeth beg
and we throb forcefully with all the intimacy
of reproducing ourselves in the act that will not.
In the sweat of it all, despite ideology, we shut out
the current events of the afternoon.

A few miles from my office a boat capsizes,
excreting three hundred men and woman
into the frigid undertow toward death
or clean prison clothing and free legal assistance.
They are not poor by their own standards
and not all the same—teacher, peasant, entrepreneur.
What they fled was a state of dreaming
to the object of that illusion, as thousands before them,
millions behind. One states he is ambitious.
Another admits he's made *a grave error.*
As their bus glides through Flushing will they see
the American destitute housed in cardboard boxes?

Outside my building, I can't look the man in the eye
who asks for *spare change.*
He smells of urine. His mouth is toothless.
Spare, Janus word for extra *and* little.
Surplus for one, dear to another. Dear young man,

there is a collective for you, a union, a regiment,
the biblical multitude of spare people,
the redundant masses of spare labor.

Come exhausted and squalid,
come shitcovered, shitfaced, diseased and immune,
dog and bitch, come third world capitalist,
come Chinese laborer whose forefathers
blew tunnels through our mountains,
lay track across our continent,
cut cane, starched the white shirts of the bourgeoisie;
whose uncle of your grandmother
fell unconscious under an avalanche of ice
in the Sierra Nevadas and could not be recovered
until the spring thaw. Come to the land of surplus value

where someone will overdose one night
after twenty hours of bussing tables. These are stories
you have not heard or if you did you translated
as propaganda to keep you poor in a poor country
as opposed to poor in a wealthy country.

I can't look in the face of the man cursing me out
because I don't want my car window washed.
I can't look at the man, empty cup, empty pant legs,
who flashes a razor at me on his tongue.
I can't speak to the girl pregnant with addiction
thanking me *for nothing*. I can
pick up the paper any day of the week
and find so much sorrow it is difficult to believe
there *are* solutions.

In the summer exhaust of a million air conditioners
I turn to my beloved for physical reassurance and simile.
The children snore softly behind the fan's whirl
because we have a place to plug in a fan.
If I turn to him, if I turn to sheafs of paper
in order to turn away from these current events
it is to revive the heartbeat of commitment.
I know poetry cannot save
but it fuels the gut that is able.

The Unbearable Heart

After Mother died, objects did not look the same. A coffee
cup had a different quality—a different tone.

Then when *The Unbearable Heart* came out, a writer friend
remarked how the mother appeared absent in my earlier
books. Not that she didn't exist but that she was always—
what?—as if in another room. And now, he continued, she
truly is gone.

A piano bench of notes.

A pier of parataxis.

The Unbearable Heart's cento

For forty-nine days after her own mother's death, she did not eat meat. *I didn't know, Mother, I'm sorry, I did not know.*

The sudden scent spills from her handbag—leather, floral lotion, mints, coins. I cannot stand.

Cuttings she had placed in tumblers on kitchen and bathroom shelves still offer their fragile roots.

I learned to swim in a mossy lake, the fish bumping my ankles like dust. The algae dotted my hair. A harmless snake writhed in the reeds.

It is odd that some words for beautiful objects sound nauseating, like *magnolia*, unlike the lovely *night soil*.

I hear a starling caught in the chimney.

The children notice their grandfather has taken off his wedding ring.

The air smells of garlic.

The girls ask unending questions—
When we breathe will Grandma become a part of us?
When we take the ferry will she come home with us?
When we're sick will she still take care of us?

I imagine watching her clip the stems off flowers / under the faucet, drop an aspirin in the vase. (Heartvine?)

(*Heartvine*, Chapter Nine in *The Tale of Genji*—)

My fingers smell of garlic.

Some days I have a thought to write down but let it go.

Garlic?

What did she say to Gustave and Max?

How do you know it's a starling?

What are the differences between dock, jetty, wharf, and pier?

The Toll Attendant

whiter under a fluorescent halo,
horn-rimmed and high-pitched
collects our coins and gives directions
to the hospital, where mother's body
may be retrieved at our earliest convenience,
to a land perpetually 3:20 am
rain always raining heavily
and to where her two daughters and two sons-in-law
travel in the family station wagon
to tell father mother is gone.
The toll attendant points beyond the plaza lights
into the dark that will become the hospital.
And when we reach the emergency room, father smiles
glad someone will finally assure him
Maude is all right.

The Stray

Father, Tomie and I stand at the hospital window
to look beyond our lives without Mother
and see a stray calico dart into rubbish.
There is something there it wants.

The River and the Lights

I cannot see the river as I drive along it
nor the bridge though its sharp lights
pierce through the humid air.
The flowering cherry and apple trees
appear as phantoms wafting in the night
under the yellow lamps.
I drive away from the funeral arrangements,
from the constant scent of mother in every
box and basket father rummages through.
Even outside buying a newspaper, he pauses at the jeweler's
noting what would become her.
Or weeding the lawn he expects her to kneel beside him
in the crabgrass. The air outside distracts me.
It is thick as the incense that will saturate our hair and best clothes
as we listen to the Lotus Sutra
an incantation recited for thousands of years.
I could drive on this parkway for hours
but I am here under the anxious restaurant signs of Manhattan
where I am the mother of two daughters
as my mother was the mother of two daughters.
I must park, climb the stairs and turn the key to my floor-through,
a light on in every room.

The Unbearable Heart

In the train an hour along the Sound, distant from the details of grief
I look up from the news toward the salt marshes
clumped beneath a snow we thought we would not see this year;
snow fallen twice this past week since mother died, instantly, 10:35 pm,
broadsided by an Arab kid fleeing a car of white kids with baseball bats;
a snow only matched by my father's head as I reach to touch him
as I have never touched him. He wishes
he could see her once more, to say goodbye,
as Ted and I said goodbye to the body that was Mother's.
Grief comes in spasms: the smell of banana bread, I think of the rotting fruit
my sister and I tossed before father came home from Yonkers General.
A flashlight. The flashlight she bought my youngest daughter
who always rummaged for the one under grandpa's side of the mattress.
The orange day lilies the florist sent to our apartment:
the lilies from the woods she brought to my wedding.

And after I told my six-year-old, Grandma died in the accident,
after tears and questions, she suggested, maybe now is a good time
to explain what the man has to do with babies.
So, I chose one perfect lily from that vase
and with the tip of a paring knife slit open the pistil
to trace the passage pollen makes to the egg cell—
the eggs I then slipped out and dotted on her fingertip, the greenish-white
translucent as the air in this blizzard that cannot cool the unbearable heart.

As I write this, I still demand your attention, Mother.

And now that she's gone how do we find her—
especially my small daughters who will eventually recall their grandmother
not as a snapshot in the faults of the mind
but as the incense in their hair long after the reading of the Lotus Sutra.

A Circle of Lanterns

Walking through a light rain
that quenches even the pavement
we turn from the funeral service
toward a Chinese banquet where
we will eat tofu and vegetables
prepared in seven different ways.
En route my older child asks
why Grandma's body was not at the temple
and I am cornered by her need for explanation:

"Because Grandma wished to be cremated.
After death the body can't feel anything—"
"Like hair?"
"Yes, like hair. So the body
is placed in a special fire
that releases the spirit, leaving only ashes.
Grandma's ashes are in a box at the temple."
She is silent, then:
"Some people say dead people are reborn."
"Some people believe that. I believe
Grandma is now wind, sunlight and moonlight."
After dinner she adds, "And mist."

The reverend explains that the Bon Festival this July
will be our mother's hatsu bon: the first time
we dress in kimono, pin up our hair and rouge our cheeks
to dance under the circle of lanterns for her
as she taught me in Kahului when I was four.
When I was ready to learn everything.

The Fragrance

Father says he would do anything to retrieve her—
the kind of bargain in folk tales where the Sweet Beauty
is returned in exchange for a famine that razes the countryside.
And yet, what hell is this where every article
emits the fragrance of Mother's cold cream.

Four Weeks After Mother's Funeral

my sister tells me that she has sat on pillows
and wept all day
giving me a kind of permission
to weep without stopping for what seems hours.
My body shakes.
I cannot catch my breath.
Ted circles his palm on my back
as if polishing wood.
After I collapse into sleep
our younger daughter cries out from her bed
to tell us of a nightmare she cannot recall.

The Hemisphere: Kuchuk Hanem

an excerpt

> Flaubert's encounter with an Egyptian courtesan produced a widely influential model of the Oriental woman. . . . He spoke for and represented her.
>
> —Edward Said, *Orientalism*

I am four. It is a summer midafternoon, my nap finished. I cannot find her. I hear the water in the bathroom. Not from the faucet but occasional splashes. I hear something like a bar of soap fall in. I cannot find her.

Flaubert's encounter—

I stand outside the white door. Reflected in the brass knob I see my face framed by a black pixie-cut. More splashes.

Flaubert's encounter, Flaubert's encounter—

I hear humming. It is mother's voice in the bathroom through the closed door and it is midafternoon. No light from beneath the door. I twist the knob and hang my weight to pull it open. In the half-light I see mother sitting in the bath: the white porcelain, gray, the yellow tiles, gray. Her hair is coiled and pinned up.

I see her breasts above the edge of the tub. I have never seen my mother without her clothes. I see her nipples.

"[S]he never spoke of herself, she never represented her emotions, presence, or history. [*Flaubert*] spoke for and represented her." [Said]

Her nipples appear dark and round. They are funny and beautiful. I leave, maybe to lie down on my pillow or find my bear. What did she say to me? Did she scold? Laugh? Just smile or ignore me? My breasts have never looked like those breasts.

"He was foreign, comparatively wealthy, male and these were historical facts of domination that allowed him not only to possess Kuchuk Hanem physically but to speak for her and tell his readers in what way she was 'typically Oriental.'" [Said]

Flaubert? In 1850, a woman with skin the color of sand in the shade of the Sphinx, midday, meant little and of course mine was seen more than veiled and I could earn a living "dancing." What I liked best were gifts of chocolate. Usually from a French man thinking I'd consider the evening amorous and reduce the rate. Paris must be lovely but for the French.

Maybe I want a cock. Maybe that's why I love sitting on an outstretched man and, his prick between my legs, rubbing it as if it were mine. Maybe that's why I love to put a cock in my mouth, feel it increase in size with each stroke, each lick, each pulse. Taste the Red Sea. Look over or up and see the man barely able to contain himself then find him pulling on my nipples or burying his tongue into my Persian Gulf. And, barely able to contain my own swell. Maybe it's my way to possess a cock. For a moment feel hegemonic and Western.

I have an addiction to silk and chocolate—gold a little. But coins are a necessity. Now chocolate—if there's a plate of chocolate, I cannot stop my hand. I tell the Nubian to store them in a cool place. I will sniff them out, as they are pungent as a garlic bulb. I will find her fingerprints on the sweaty sweets.

We both use our mouths, professionally.

> "My heart begins to pound everytime I see [a prostitute] in low-cut dresses walking under the lamplight in the rain, just as monks in their corded robes have always excited some deep ascetic corner of my soul . . . " [Flaubert's letters]

Maybe it's my way to possess a cock. For a moment feel hegemonic and Western.

It's true when all is said and done, I am less a dancer than a whore. Men pay me money, stick their cocks in me, laugh, weep, curse, or silently ride my body. And leave. That's what I am, a whore and alone. To be despised by the men because who else would let them come as they come but someone with vagrant morals. Despised by wives, mistresses, and fiancées for my abilities, independence, the peculiar attention that I receive. I am scorned by the religious. By the courts and by my parents. But I do not fear a man's departure. *Know that.*

I have become a continent. I have become a hemisphere.

> *"Kuchuk Hanem is a tall, splendid creature, lighter in coloring than an Arab . . . slightly coffee-colored. When she bends, her flesh ripples into bronze ridges . . . her black hair, wavy, unruly, pulled straight back on each side from a center parting beginning at the forehead; small braids joined together at the nape of the neck. She has one upper incisor, right, which is beginning to go bad."* [Flaubert]

A garlic bulb

The female body as imperialist colony is not a new symbol. Sexual impulse as revolutionary impulse? Do women depend upon the sexual metaphor for identity, an ironic figure of speech? Will I fall into the trap of writing from an imperialist point of view? From a patriarchal one? How can we write erotica and not? What would an anti-imperialist framework look like? And, weren't women the original keepers of lineage? Of narrative?

Can I speak for her? For the Turkish, Nubian, the—brown, black, blacker?

> *"Coup with Safia Zugairah—I stain the divan. She is very corrupt and writhing, extremely voluptuous. But the best was the second copulation with Kuchuk. Effect of her necklace between my teeth. Her cunt felt like rolls of velvet as she made me come."* [Flaubert]

Her name, talents, and shaved cunt have outlived her person. We remember her for the dance and the fuck. For the hemisphere created. But what would she have said? Could the words be translated?

What did she say to Gustave or Max?

The way I wish mother to speak up so I can become a woman.

The way nothing is verbatim.

The way she peels and slices a garlic bulb—

I hear her pour coffee. Open the refrigerator for milk. Walk without slippers to the living room, to a stack of magazines with cakes on the covers.

I hear her pour two cups of coffee.

I hear her chopping vegetables. Garlic.

I remember him not for the sex but for the cool shower we took after 3 am. Holding and twisting each other under the hard spray, laughing at the cold. We powdered under the fan before I gently pushed him to the door. To go home. To his wife. If he has one.

I am so hungry. I consume Said.

The men want me, Flaubert wanted me, not for the sex but for the experience . . . and especially the sadness he recovers in departure. He knows he will not return once he leaves Esna for Turkey. But I know he will return (that's why he came in the first place, to never leave) perhaps in the sound of rain, invisible in the night. It may not snow in Esna but I know it rains in Paris.

Or the garlic she sliced.

The garlic.

I smell the pungency all night on my fingers.

My sister and I often go to the beach by ourselves. I bring a transistor to connect myself to the rest of the world. One afternoon, as I lay on my towel, a short wiry man in a small aqua swimsuit walked over and asked to sit beside me. He didn't speak much English but conveyed that he was a sailor from Portugal. Swarthy. In hindsight probably mid-twenties. By way of conversation, he pointed to a large tattoo on his arm; an intricately inked geisha, after Utamaro. He smiled as if, somehow, I identified with this. I did a little. He asked if I'd like to board his ship.

The evening my sister and I ate by ourselves at Jack-in-the-Box, I forgot our money and had to return to the hotel. Around the corner I ran past a man rubbing his protruding cock. Another time on a bus, a man sat across from us, his cock sticking out of his shorts' pant leg—and he covered and exposed it with his cap. Pitiful belongings.

What would Kuchuk Hanem say if I were to sit beside her in the predawn, tobacco wafting into our hair like the memory of my first husband studying for finals. The fragrance of a coffee as rich as the mud from the Nile that must flood the fields to award farmers a relatively easy season. The thick silt coating the land, the throat, the tongue. Sheer caffeine heightening the ultramarine tiles as we turn toward one another. Would she have offered to put on her veil and go out herself to the market for figs or ask her slave to fetch a basket of them?

Would she offer me figs and ask me to *stay* or tell me to *get the hell out, what's a married woman doing here—curious? You looking for someone? You want lessons? You want me? It must mean something that our hearts are cut by men like a dress pattern but sewn by women.*

Who is the cartographer?

Flaubert's encounter—

What is my stake in this—?

> *"[Dear Louise,] the oriental woman is no more than a machine: she makes no distinction between one man and another man. Smoking, going to the baths, painting her eyelids and drinking coffee—such is the circle of occupations within which . . ."* [Flaubert]

After I dice the garlic, spread it around the crackling oil, I can smell it on my fingers. Even after I wash my hands for dinner. Even while I'm eating fried rice. Even after nibbling chocolate.

Even after washing the children. Walking the dog.

"... within which her existence is confined. As for physical pleasure, it must be very slight, since the well-known button, the seat of same, is sliced off at an early age ..." [Flaubert]

Even after slicing garlic—

Even after reading Said—

"[Louise, you tell me] that Kuchuk's bedbugs degrade her in your eyes; for me they were the most enchanting touch of all. Their nauseating odor mingled with the scent of her skin which was dripping with sandalwood oil ..." [Flaubert]

We powder by the window before I firmly push him to the door. To go home under the stars that vanish when you stare.

My bad tooth aches. I'll walk to the baths for a soak—

Flaubert's encounter—

No light from under the door. I hear splashes. What did she say to me? Did she scold? Laugh? Just smile or ignore me?

My mother would have told me the story of Kuchuk Hanem, but she died suddenly three months ago.

Earshot

(1992)

When I think of a piano, I think of a quote from Ralph Ellison's "A Song of Innocence": "They say that folks misuse words, but I see it the other way around, words misuse people. Usually when you think you're saying what you mean you're really saying what the words want you to say. It's just like a drunk piano player I know who says that when he's drinking he plays where his fingers take him. Well, once upon a time they took him straight into the biggest church in town and got him thrown in jail for playing 'Funky Butt' on the god-box, which is Mr. Fats Waller's name for the pipe organ. One never knows, *do* one, as he used to say."

Ralph and Fanny. Mom and Dad were so pleased to be friends with them. And I inherited a dress that she'd given Mother ("Ralph thought the colors too—what? gaudy for her?").

Earshot, a cento

The man next door / paints / *C O W* / on all his animals. / It's deer season.

Here the mind deregulates language.

Groin sounds like grown. / Groan.

Revolution / is the soft / exact / orbit of planet, moon, seed. / Also seizing the means of production / for our class.

Here I will not argue with God / because who can be certain there is an Ear / or what form the Ear may take: tree trunk, / bassinet, dog shit, potato, star?

Here I asked, *What did the afterbirth look like?*

like *cardinal, blue jay, wren?*

Clover, lavender, wisteria, thistle—

Here I recall the constellation glued to the ceiling and,

while cleaning, I thought / how rust felt like his face in the morning.

Here he meant that much to me while // I organized a reading for Ernesto Cardenal— / which hall would hold 1,000 people / which day and hour to attract 1,000.

It was deer season when my mind turned bale into *bale* into *bail*.

And when the miner pulled up the canary cage—

the cardinal, cardinal, wren

Revolutions

Forbidden to learn Chinese
the women wrote in the language
of their islands
and so Japanese
became the currency of high aesthetics
for centuries
as did the female persona: the pine
the longing. This is the truth.

(We can rise above those needles.)

The red silk from my grandmother
amazes me. Think of the peasant
immigrating from rice fields
to black volcanic soil. The black beaches.
The children black
in this sunlight
against the parents' will or aspirations.

(Anywhere else
girls of mixed marriages would be prostitutes or courtesans.)

I want those words
that gave women de facto power,
those religious evocations: dreams so potent
'she became pregnant' or 'men killed'
or 'the mistress died in pain.'
I connect to that century
as after breath is knocked out
we suck it back in.

The words the men stole after all
to write about a daughter's death
or their own (soft) thigh
belongs to us—to me—
though translation is a border
we look over or into;
sometimes a familiar noise
("elegant confusion"). But can *meaning*
travel
the way capital moves
like oil in the Alaskan pipeline
or in tankers in the Strait of Hormuz?
Can those sounds move like that?
Yes. But we don't understand.

But we don't know
what it means to speak frankly
even to ourselves. Patricia,
fertility is not the antithesis of virility.
I can't help it.

If I could translate the culture
women cultivate
I would admit to plum
and plumb.

I always begin with a season.
Like: snow and plums in the wooden bowl
make me love him. How
I warm one in my fist

then lick it until the skin
grows so tender it bursts
beneath my breathing.
The yellow is bright.
The snow is warm.

Some of our lessons issue from song
because there are never enough
older sisters
especially from the South via Detroit
where we look for a model
with the desperation of a root—
where a bride is a state—
where *heat lightning* is pronounced:
lie down on my breast
so your tongue and teeth reach my tit
and I can—
where *yes*—

I didn't learn poetic diction from the Classics,
rather, transistor radios. Confidence
in my body also. After years—
the confidence that gives and gives
and is not afraid to take either.
Exploring the words means plunging down
not skimming across
or watching whitecaps however lovely.
Not balking at fear either:
the walls are filled with sounds,
the windows, with sorrow.

Revolution for example is the soft
exact
orbit of planet, moon, seed.
Also seizing the means of production
for our class.
Where did that come from?
It all begins with women, she said.

Like the warp and woof of cloth.

Like how there's no "free verse" so we'll search
for the subtle structures: the poetic closure,
the seven kinds of ambiguity, etc.

Not tonight, dear.

How it's not so sad really
for a husband or wife
to come alone.

Komachi's reputation came from legend:
the 99th time a lover visited her door
(the night before she would let him enter)
he died.

That's the breaks.

In a patriarchy is such cruelty *cruelty*
or survival? Is the father also to blame
for ugly daughters? for the unruly ones?

Come sit by the radiator and open window.
When the baby hiccoughed inside her
her whole body shook.

Afterbirth is not a time or reform
it belongs to a separation we turn toward.

Comp. Lit.

after Murasaki Shikibu's Genjimonogatari

i.

You barely remember Japanese.
But in this volume
a half-light matches your palm.
Moist. Beige. Silken.
Genji would never saturate his silk
with incense. Any of the purples
remind him of Murasaki
the first time he saw her
with a basket of sparrows.
Her childish voice chirps.
What happens when there are two texts
in translation?
Who can we trust
when our *bungo* has deteriorated
to elementary tables
for *beshi, kemu, gotoshi.*
How can we compare
without the original:

> *When shall I see it lying in my hand, the young grass of the moorside*
> *that springs from purple roots?*
> Arthur Waley

> *I long to have it, to bring it in from the moor,*
> *The lavender that shares it roots with another.*
> Edward Seidensticker

The purple reminds him of Murasaki
who reminds him of his stepmother
who he loves in place of his mother.
He could bury his face between her breasts
and pull her nipples from the layers of silk
until she cries out
in a whisper close to pain.

ii.

Why my interest in Genji?

The little girl makes advances on the quilt.
He gently pushes her away
and presents a lacquered hand mirror
from a bed stand.
She still has it
though cannot recall the rewarded moment.
And he still recalls its other uses,
framing genitals or complexions.

The reader will not find this in any text.

He wanted to be her father
but did not know what it meant
to be in trust of her adoration and anger,
the one opening her narrative.

iii.

With many timid glances toward him she began to write. Even the
childish manner in which she grasped the brush gave him a thrill of
delight which he was at a loss to explain.

    AW

It was strange that even her awkward, childish way of holding the
brush should so delight him.

    ES

Chirp, chirp, chirp, she said.
Translation?
Where do the translators translate?
New York? Tokyo? Kyoto?
At their desk? tatami? longhand?
Can we go from stroke to scribble?
And who are *they*?
When you turn your back
will they laugh
because you forgot your *bungo*;
can't even understand the entry
—let alone the kanji—
not so much to discern
but to correspond
from her small heart.
He needed to surround this muscle
like a second rib cage.
Each night when he looked in on her
his black hair blended with the night.
He would give her any toy or garment or food.

He would find snow for her.
He would be sure she understood the necessity
for perfect brush strokes,
fresh, agile.
Fat like an infant's leg.
Her legs.
Cheeks. Waist.
Like a boy
he could move through any compartment in the court
with a vague sense of home.

> The little girl was at first terribly frightened. She did not know what
> he was going to do with her and shuddered violently. Even the feel of
> his delicate, cool skin when he drew her to him gave her gooseflesh.
>
> AW

> Genji pulled a singlet over the girl, who was trembling like a leaf.
>
> ES

He would surround her heart
so she would surround his
with her little pool of carp.
How he envied her playmates
all holding hands at the Tanabata Festival.

iv.

The translator's subjectivity
makes the parts whole: a saucer and cup.
Hot water.
She sounded like a bird

chirping in the garden or corridor
and looked like one
with little pink wings and white feet
flitting among the ladies.
What would she like from him?
A container of fireflies.
He smiled. Of course—
recalling how he used one to spark
an illicit meeting—
and had kimonos and dolls sewn anyway.
Friend. Father.
Husband.
Why are some birds so brightly colored?
she asked him.
If he could keep her this young—
but in learning verse
she would need to know the brighter feathers.
He enjoyed seeing the colors of his men
through the trees and mist—
imagined a woman looking and seeing a familiar face
as a branch blew aside,
the underside of leaves pale as tissue.
She would ask him for things like a cup
for her dolls.
Pinecones.
She became the translation
and so did he.
For me the translation of figures became a fragrance,
kaoru—
as the author, Murasaki, designed—
so distinct one could taste it in one's throat.

He was the father who didn't leave.
The mother who didn't die.
She could bring her dolls to him
when he came home.

v.

She wrote with such childish abandon
that errors took on a style.
To make her his.
What would this mean:
wait a few years and put aside her toys,
replace them with strips of paper,
feel her crushed beneath him.
Why did a woman write this?
Did she speak from the small heart,
her name her name also?
Clover, lavender, wisteria, thistle—
black carp.
He locks her into womanhood.
She grows to need him,
tolerate him and become the adversary
of all other women.
Is this the translation:
the way women who need one another
are placed at odds for men.
Is this one of the lessons
that scrolls out from the many days on her knees
writing and rewriting.
A screen. To screen.
Do I survey from the male persona?

vi.

That this was what Genji had long been wanting came to her as a complete surprise and she could not think why he should regard the unpleasant thing that had happened last night as in some way the beginning of a new and more intimate friendship between them.
AW

She had not dreamed he had anything of the sort in mind. What a fool she had been, to repose her whole confidence in so gross and unscrupulous a man.
ES

vii.

Omitted chapter
AW

It was chiefly because [the Third Princess] found [Genji's] attentions so distasteful that she became a nun. She had hoped that she might now find peace—and [yet] here he was with [his] endless regrets. She longed to withdraw to a retreat of her very own, but she was not one to say so.
ES

viii.

The translator puts the pen down
and stretches his arms and neck.
Genji is complete.
He's completed the text

in time for the fall semester.
The students call him professor and bore him
but bring a salary, medical benefits, an office.
The volumes of translation are exact.
Exactly right.
He walks into the bathroom,
turns off the light and sits down.

ix.

Genji looked behind every screen
for the one who resembled his mother,
for his mother,
yet did not understand that the mother
would always be dead
and always be someone he'd adore
with a passion reserved for lovers;
that he would annotate each woman
like a chapter returned to again and again;
that each *scene*
would be an attempt to reach out of infancy
because the breast is always a breast.
Indeed, his second wife, Murasaki,
resembled his stepmother who he loved
and who it is said resembled his real mother.
Women surrounded him like a nest
with their bodies, fragrances,
spirits—
but could not complete his search.

The Heat

Did you watch women collect red seaweed
in the white foam
and think of afternoons in your apartment
view of fire escape and brick wall,
smell of everyone's cooking,
taste of each other's mouth and extremities.
Did you listen to their work song and think of the radio in the alley blaring
undying love, love, undying love.
The air was full of air,
the heat, heart.
From Ono no Komachi
we know one can travel in dreams.
The difference between the dreamer
and the dream traveler noted in
a broken twig, footprints in the garden,
or the doormat muddy and askew.
Yes.
Any effort at love
resolved itself in fucking and crying.
I imagine you turning away on your Harley
toward the urban blight.
*

It was Danceteria in December.
I think I leaned over to tell you
I wanted another drink
but licked your ear to my own surprise.
More in the taxi.
We couldn't believe it:
discovering the edge of heat
that makes a person lie to everyone
yet never admit it even as the words unravel.

I could play *mother* with you:
a naked baby I'd nurse and rock
then suddenly we were adults again
on top of orgasm.

I could refuse to disrobe
until finally, your hand up my skirt,
drenched and crying
we'd give in to bludgeoning throbs.

Or the little hand mirror
held like a keyhole
as we watched something *in another room*
distant and glistening.

Even rising to leave for my husband
the blood could not calm.

*

Sometimes I don't know I'm writing a poem.

*

Meeting a year later
I could barely look at you.
Now I have enough distance to ask questions
beyond ember:
What was my need to leave the nuptial bed
for a single, dark in the afternoon?
A need akin to leaving a father?
That departure we think makes me, *me.*
One looks up from a newspaper
and knows some chest or ass
is it

then goes beyond imagination
and still doesn't call it wrong (was it?)
calls it *need*—
as absolute as a child running across the schoolyard
away from the figure in herring-bone tweed.
There are times
when I think existence
could not be without the excruciating melt
of reason
or the acute sorrow of separation.
Is the self so persistent,
her self,
one thinks she doesn't look for a mother
even at the point of telling some bitch to *fuck off*
he's mine. I said mine,
honey.
*

This summer fishermen catch enormous fish,
fins rotting from the diseased waters
we vacation in,
syringes stuck in the sand.
*

I have to admit I miss your letters
pungent from the crack seed
you rolled around your mouth,
the waitresses I know you leaned against,
the quotes from Wittgenstein,
and somehow from the whales—
your letters, letter perfect from the rewriting.
I know you too well—

down to the angle of your hard-on.
Yes, the texture.
But why did I risk everything for the heat?
Was it because there was an alternative *everything*?
One that included hours of quoting Donne
instead of eating and drinking.
One where pleasure included difficult questions
about our individual futures and American literature.
As I write I lapse into—
here, here is my envelope, baby.

*

Say it. *Betrayal*:
1.) springing from the uterus,
2.) rejecting the breast for a view of the world, new tastes, society,
3.) demanding the babysitter,
4.) demanding daddy,
5.) and later, replacing daddy with boyfriends.
Of course, it's all point of view:
betrayal to one
development to the child.

*

Whenever I ask the neighbor's little girl
if she wants this or that
she says, *I want something else.*
Of course.

*

It's a relief, though not a conclusion, to visit you now
and not taste desire from teeth to gut.
To know we've come full spiral:
just to ensure tough standards in one another's work

even as I recall the afternoon I said *no*
and you threatened to tie me to your desk
then kicked me out shouting: *save it for your fucking poems*—
what was that stranger music?
*

I could go on.

Foreclosure

Sand

When I write I feel like a mother
after one grows older and feels *older than mother*.

Or I feel like the shore in early April
when the light becomes lighter.

China

I've been looking for you, Mother,
since my breasts first appeared.
Where did I learn to speak to other women
with these awkward hands
or protect myself?
If I could protect myself
without smoothing this tablecloth
or letting him or him order dinner,
the nausea might settle
into relief from daughter to bride.
The suitor also felt good in control
as if that included bronze, sand,
porcelain, fucking
our brains out and the comforter—
the comfort of mother having read till you fell asleep.
Why did you ask her
to reread the endings over and over—

he packed up his cooking-stove and went away
in the direction of—

I had to be taught at twenty-four
to say *no.*
Not *sorry,* not *perhaps later*
but *nosogetthefuckouttamyface, jack.*

To dismantle indirection,
to take into my own hands
sleep and awake,
childhood and child,
must the father learn to say *woman.*

Transistors

Fortunately, her stories prepared me for everything:
men who always perished, men who never expired,
stepsisters and talking animals.

With such tokens even blemishes
or the absence of bouquets
would be less thorny.

I could look into my reflection,
say my own name as if someone else spoke
and realize *that's her all right*

then graduate to the girls from Detroit or London
the bad girls
who instructed in usages of yes: *baby baby oh baby*

Wren

The father's needs eclipsed our own aviary—
cardinal, blue jay, wren.
On tv the man said:
Don't go into the mine
without a mask.
When we pulled up the cage of canaries
they were dead.

Finches are yellow, too, aren't they?
I remember the time a finch pecked at our window
then flew in, a little tag on its claw.
Father let me hold it softly.

I wish the daughter could be angry and still be a daughter.

Airport

She couldn't remain on the island
in the little dirt town with no cinema
and barely a dance hall.
She wished herself to Chicago
and there reinvented herself
on the *L*. I wish I could go
on break from these patterns. Conjure
leaves, rose, pine, hedges. But
where does an arrangement come from—
I just don't know. Perhaps
from this snapshot:
Honolulu Airport, 1947,

a young woman with permed hair,
high heels, a beige suit,
and even though black-and-white
obvious red lipstick.
Nothing *Japanese*.
If only she'd given a signal:
it's all right to have breasts.

The Izu Dancer

an excerpt

In time we belong to what the objects mean—
as when, around 2 am, the stomach sours from all the coffee.
And when the character strokes blur into the mess of lines and noises
they really are. Though in some respects the ideograms
are astonishingly plain:

tree   木   forest   森

woman   女   mischief; noisy; assault   姦

But the complex unfolding of a single sentence
where the subject was lost somewhere inside—
baffled, humiliated, and toughened my spirit.
I persevered in my search for the fragrance of words
in this modest story—the only Kawabata story I could read.
Where did he unearth

不自然な程美しい黒髪が私の胸に触れそうになった。

("Her hair, so rich it seemed unreal, almost brushed against my chest.")
Where did I find the hands on my shoulders, sliding down my arms
then up under my t-shirt, into my bra,
squeezing my breasts, pinching my nipples so hard
I blinked to hold back tears.
He watched my expression as a meteorologist reads delicate instruments.
If the body is a map, a weather map, summer vacations or winter holidays
all begin here. Something a student may not realize.

Daylilies on the Second Anniversary of My Second Marriage

Watching the daylilies
shrivel by afternoon,
the buds behind them
swollen from green to orange,
I think of our wedding
two years ago.
Mother brought armfuls
from the woods near their home.
She told me
in China they dry the blossoms
and eat them in soup.
I imagine the spent lilies
opening a second time
in the hot broth.

The New Parents

Setting aside her rattle and doll
you stretch across our bed
and draw me over you.
I curve in, pulsing
till my breasts spot your chest with milk.

The Calf

A day like any other, my brother and I were debating,
in this case, the possibility of the U.S. employing
limited nuclear weapons to force Saddam to his knees,
the repercussions to Kuwait and ultimately
the cash flow back into India.
As we walked through the family's nursery business
we realized the ten thousand rose bushes
looked changed, looked dying.
Turning the leaves and buds in our fingers
we checked for something familiar, disease or insect,
then tested and found the well water
thoroughly polluted by a new chemical factory.
Think of our horror imagining the children especially
drinking and bathing in this toxic stuff.
So, we organized with neighbors and, long story
short, marched on government offices.
Eventually you know the company installed
a pipeline and treatment plant. A victory to be sure.
But now our Citizen's Watch focuses
twenty miles outside central Hyderabad
on Patancheru. Once a farming community,
now *a rapid industrialization zone*, Patancheru
is one of the most polluted places on this planet.
I do not exaggerate. One can witness the results
of industrialization—which I don't oppose in theory—
results without the political will to control *side effects*.
Imagine two thousand acres of fertilized land saturated
with sulfides, sulfates, nitrites, nitrates and phosphorous,
the subsoil contaminated one hundred forty-five feet,
yet people drink this *water* for lack of other sources.
Imagine cattle and goats dying from quenching their thirst.

I saw a calf born without skin.
I met people suffering mental disorders
from chemicals blocking sufficient oxygen to the brain.
Children die of leukemia—unheard of
before these three hundred factories
began dumping industrial waste in public places. Imagine
children developing open sores from playing in the dirt
—just the sifting and tumbling children do—
I saw a calf born without skin.
Why an outlying village has no children at all
because the women repeatedly miscarry.
I tell you I am not against industry
but it must benefit people not industry itself.
I saw a calf born without skin.
There very well could be a link between local policies
and what some call *an international network of capitalism.*
Rose bushes are one thing but a *miscarriage.*
I tell you—I saw a calf born without skin.
You know Americans say that for Indians life is cheap,
that such problems lie with Indian mismanagement,
but more to the point, labor is cheap here for the West.
Further, who spends a billion dollars a day
to bomb a small country even neglecting its own people
for the sake of *a new world order.* Imagine
a calf without skin. What is chemical warfare
when women become sterile just drinking water
or, after bathing in well water,
abort masses that resemble the human heart.
If I sound defensive it's because I'm tired sometimes.
I saw a calf born. I teach full time, help out in the nursery
and organize with the Citizen's Watch.

I saw a calf. Born. Without skin.
I'm tired and I hope it isn't from the toxins—a calf
without skin—toxins leaking again
from the now-broken pipeline.
I saw a calf born without skin. I saw a calf born without skin.
There's a saying something like:
there's the battle and there's the war.

From my interviews for Bill Brand's film *Coalfields* (see *Volatile*):

"The solicitor didn't want me to break it down, and talk about that the lungs is like a sponge. Therefore it got crevices in it. And this sand dust, rock dust, coal dust, mixing and getting in there and it's cement in there. They tried to wash it out years ago by putting a little hose down in there in the guy's lungs and that was drowning people. They couldn't do it that way because that sets up infection. Packed in there just like cement. This is the problem of pneumoconiosis. That this infection just stayed there and then it turned black. It just turned black like coal. And all the pressure were in the veins and the blood pass through all that is petrified. It overworks the heart and causes a heart condition. The heart stops. They didn't want me to say that you see." Fred Carter

"Carter was taking me and twelve other men to Abington, Virginia to get a blood gas test. What we didn't know was that there was an FBI man sitting in this vehicle with us.... and I kept wondering about this guy because he didn't talk to us, he listened. He was a real good listener. He didn't talk like a coal miner. He didn't look like a coal miner, he didn't act like a coal miner, and when we went to eat he wouldn't even sit with us." Bill Thompson

Seams

The Coalfields *Project, text two*

The seam was gray as a recollection
of the maps and typewriter,
of the apartment door I closed
on my husband as I said, *sorry*—
Gray as the morning air
in Dupont City full of *Dupont*.
Gray as my hope to use this assignment
in another state to ruminate and move on—
That Thursday was my day
to not talk about Fred Carter's case.
To interview Blue, an unemployed coal miner,
who drove me around
pulling over to pick up coffee,
adjust the windshield wipers—
and I felt sadder for the red
than the raw yellow
in the hills. How to take
this virility (*yes*) in my heart
—the politics
that make my blood surge—
and place it in the feminine land:
the seams, drift mouth,
strip mines, hollers.
So, on a steamy autumn day
I could smell something like
Ortho cream or rubber
except it was Dupont
a late Thursday afternoon.
Was it this female
that forced the men to tender moments

(even art)
in the shafts
or made me hope Fred into saying
whereas the lungs are like a sponge
even as the Company
invades his very alveoli.
If I could be a virile woman
I would be these sorry hills
separate and gorgeous
where the plain language
(*black lung*)
becomes stripped.
Where the thin-seam miner
guts the side of a mountain.
Where some men cut open some kid's stomach
in the parking lot
for being black with a white girl.
That, too, this landscape.
Also, that day—watching coal
pour out the tipple—
was so exquisite
I just sat in the car.
Some moments I stopped breathing
as rain sprayed through the window
across my cheek and sweater.
Fred would never last a week in jail
and they know it. I knew
I was home
when I mistook *mantrip* for *mantrap.*
The men winked and offered

wanna go down?
I grinned—*a couple inches or a few yards?*
That made them ask,
where you from anyway?
Between sass and conversations with Blue
on how he got his name
when the other miners threw him out of the shower
into the snow—a kind of hazing—
and how he paints while he watches the tv
and the kids
and how I write on the subways—
I knew this gray would hurt
every time I opened my grip.
He'll never come home.
Fred would have a heart attack
in that hole.
Miners never die of natural causes
in the lungs of the South—
in Dupont City, Marytown, Ellenboro,
Coal Fork, Burning Spring, Nitro.

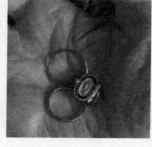

Air Pocket

(1989)

Dara collected my epigraphs for a piece in *jubilat* and I was so grateful to see them in a kind of "Extracts"—or zuihitsu.

Rudyard Kipling came first: "But the Parsee came down from his palm tree, wearing his hat, from which the rays of the sun were reflected in more-than-oriental splendour, packed up his cooking-stove, and went away in the direction of Orotavo, Amygdala, the Upland Meadows of Anantarivo, and the Marshes of Sonoput."

"How the Rhinoceros Got His Skin" was one of the Golden Books that I'd ask Mother to read repeatedly. At one point— and I am not sure how I figured this out—she hid *Rapunzel*. Or was it *Hansel and Gretel*? How I loved thinking about white stones in his pocket.

A pocket of assonance.

Air Pocket, a cento

Nothing eats the kimonos / in the trunk under the stairs

laughter / fills every corner / and lizards fill / the screen.

You wheel Grandfather's chair across the yard, / chickens parting, toward the porch / where Grandmother and Father played hanafuda.

Grandfather had left Hiroshima / to burn sugar cane in Maui

then found himself / torn, like fruit off a tree.

That morning he dropped his teeth in a water glass.

I'll never forget / the shower that riddled the tobacco fields . . . before Suyapa was hit by mortar.

The streets were named after martyrs, / often women: / Marta, Bertha, Ariel, Rita, Beatriz, Arlen,—

"Maude, be outraged," she whispered.

Yes, what is your weakness / becomes your strength, / calendar, identity, lawn, / rock garden, pond.

Can we sleep—birds in flight—

Seizure / you envision / as the street / after the water has broken.

And I am glad for the chance to revise the young woman's poetry. She did not have a woman to guide her in that air pocket.

Nor did she have white stones for the moonlight.

What she—what I have now is a granddaughter, Ava, who at five, asks what a soul is and what is the purpose of a soul. I ask her what she thinks, and she says that a soul is air that sleeps inside the body until the person dies and then it wakes up and is lively so people remember the person.

A story does circulate like a present. The present. And the granddaughter's stories are for her grandmother.

Bon Odori—New York, 1967

Nothing eats the kimonos
in the trunk under the stairs.
They were Grandmother's—
none for weddings, all
for dance, the sleeves fall below
our waists. We save them.
Sometimes I think *caterpillar*
or *spinning* although
I do not think of Utamaro's geisha,
paper in her teeth—not his
woodcut—rather Cassatt's drypoint,
The Letter: her head, black
hair tied back, bent forward
as she licks the envelope—
exactly like our mother.
We send letters. In winter we write
about summer. About that dusk
when we visit the temple, clap twice
in front of all those boxes,
light incense, then
collect along the river to dance
in memory of grandparents.
My kimono, the color
of mulberry leaves
with tie-dyed shapes like cocoons,
will glow in the circle
of dancers. The drummer is
always so handsome! Sleeves
and moths flutter and lanterns
sway in the heat. The drummer,
half naked, is in the center.

The Air Itself

The fire hydrants clear
and cool the soft black streets.
Arms and legs
cluster in thresholds:
I am tired.
What have we to see
or sell: teeth,
tongue, fingers, blood.
I own these. I rent three windows
and plumbing
—listen to the walls—
is that a neighbor
or water pipes? Strip
the blinds. The streetlights attract
shadows and paper bags.
I am tired. How many
colors mix to make brown,
these buildings? Touch me:
toss the blanket off the bed.
You smell like industrial glue,
vinyl, and sweat. Embrace.
Hold. I am tired. Clutch.
Forget trembling and persuade me
to feel: revolt. Begin now.
We are tired.
Gather. The air itself
suffocates this morning.

Seizure

In Nicaragua
old women
mobilize with sticks and boiling water
again.
You're North American.
You figure it's the season.
But back home
the moon
acts like that girl
who'd been fucked in so many places
she hardly knew which hole
was for babies
and you know you understand

un deber de cantar

and you know you understand
your desire
to see Broadway
NY NY
taken in a flash of July heat
and you know you want it.
(The green parrots snap
guapa
and your thighs sweat like mad.)
And you want it.
Shit. We don't have mountains here.
The rooftops will do the trick

you think out loud.

Because you belong to a process
that belongs to you

one

you love to touch

and nurse

and deploy

on your lap, here,
Nicaragua. On your

lap, here *Nueva*
New York. Here

novio. Baby
sister. When I say *mujeres*

man of course

I mean *y hombres*

también.
I'll never forget

the shower that riddled the tobacco fields
on the Honduran border of Nicaragua

where Suyapa
una nina de 4 anos

learned June 9, 1983
what *somocistas* are

—yanquis, contras—
if she didn't know

before she was hit by mortar. Seizure
you envision

as the street
after the water has broken.

Resistance: A Poem on Ikat
an excerpt

By the time the forsythia blossomed
in waves along the parkway
the more delicate cherry and apple
had blown away if you remember
correctly. Those were days
when you'd forget socks and books
after peeing in the privacy
of its branches and soft earth.
What a house you had
fit for turtles and sparrows—
like the sparrow who
wrapped in a silk kimono
wept for her tongue
clipped off by an old woman.
You'll never forget her story
or its vengeance as striking
as the yellow around your small shoulders.

   Tongue-cut-sparrow mother called her.
   And so you recognized one
   bereft of speech.
click click
   Soon came mounds of flesh
   and hair here and there.
   Centuries earlier
   you'd have been courted
or sold—
   for a Eurasian, sold.
click click
   Did Murasaki soak the cloth
   in incense

then spread it on the floor,
			did she wait there in bleached cotton,
			red silk and bare feet—
Probably not—
			Most likely not—
And you fell in love with her
deeply as only a little girl could.
Pulling at your nipples
you dreamt of her body
that would become yours.
			a becoming body
red as a Judy Chicago plate—
			likely
click click
			one man expressed his sorrow
			in a woman's voice
morning and mourning—
			" . . . when I was bathing along the shore
			scarcely screened by reeds
			I lifted my robe revealing my leg
			and more."
pink as a Judy Chicago plate—
			The cut burned
			so she flapped her wings
			and cried out
			but choked
			on blood.
(For resist dyeing, I wound the thread
so tight my fingers
turned indigo.)
			Mother said *murasaki* is *purple*

When the Shining Prince first saw
Murasaki with her little basket of sparrows
he realized he could form this child
into the one forbidden him. For that
he would persist
into old age.
 (She only wanted a bit
 of rice starch, the sparrow.)
Against dying, I tried
resistance. Of course—
 you can't resist—
The box of the sparrow's vengeance
contained evils comparable to agent orange
or the minamata disease. The old man
lived contentedly without
the old woman. But—why her?
except that she was archetypal?
 warp and woof—
click click
 click clack
Archetypes?
 —supreme archetypes—
The Supremes soothed like older sisters
rubbing your back
kissing your neck and pulling you into
Motor City, USA
and whether you realized it
or not that
was the summer
of Watts and though you
were in a one-hundred-year slumber

as far as that news
the ramifications
>   *the ramifications*
the resistance
bled through transistors
>   a *class* act
a click clack
>   Blues from indigo, reds
>   from mendoekoe root, yellows, boiling
>   tegaran wood
>   and sometimes by mudbath!
(A mudbath!)
>   Purple as a Judy Chicago plate—
Bind the thread
with hemp or banana leaves
before soaking it in the indigo
black as squid as seaweed as his hair
>   as his hair
>   as I lick his genitals
>   then take one side
>   in my mouth then the other
>   till he cries softly
>   *please*
Please
>   *yes*—
But—why the old woman?
Why not the man?
Who wrote the story—
>   who read the story—?
Who wove the threads—
>   for eons?

click click
clack clack
       Georgia O'Keeffe's orchid shocked you
       so even now you can picture the fragrance
as if braille
       as if *chirp chirp*
"Should a stranger witness the performance
he is compelled to dip his finger
into the dye and taste it. Those employed
must never mention the names of dead people
or animals. Pregnant or sick women—
       "Pregnant or sick women
       are not allowed to look on;
       should this happen they are punished
       as strangers."
chirp chirp
       "[L]anguage does not differ
       from instruments of production,
       from machines, let us say—"
from a shuttle
       the Japanese women
       wrote in Japanese
       unlike the men's
       Chinese, stale and
bloodless and
       less pliant than the female persona:
       "While I was so dejected,
       the men of the ship or the captain
       fell to singing boat songs till
       it could scarcely be borne."

Shibori, too, uses resistance—
and the white design
floats on silk
like fish eggs or ghostly nipples
      the sparrow wore a shibori sash
      tied around her waist
click
      clack
"Winter kept us warm"
      Yet, in this labor—
in this iambic labor
I imagine a daughter in my lap
who I will never give away
but see off with
      bolts
dyed with resistance.

When You Leave
the earliest apparition

This sadness could only be a color
if we call it *momoiro*, Japanese

for *peach-color,* as in the first story
Mother told us: It is the color of the hero's skin

when the barren woman discovered him
inside a peach floating down the river.

And of the banner and gloves she sewed
when he left her to battle the horsemen, then found himself

torn like fruit off a tree. Even when he met a monkey,
dog and bird, he could not release

the color he saw when he closed his eyes. In his boat
the lap of the waves against the hold

was too intimate as he leaned back to sleep. He wanted
to leave all thoughts of peach behind him—

the fruit that brought him to her
and she, the one who opened the color forever.

Did Mother fashion a sewing basket from a cigar box
for her, too? Did she include a simple pattern, chalk, and
thread?

And was each item finally a ghost? Or a ghost orchid?

Notes
for *The Ghost Forest* and *Likeness*

Notes for earlier poems appear in respective collections. These include references to periodicals and books.

The text on gray-shaded pages is a thread of comments and reflections that I have woven through the collections. Inside these are references to:

Kaga no Chiyo was a Japanese poet whose dates are 1703–1775.

Kanzuke Mineo's waka is #832 from *Kokinshū* and translated by Edward Seidensticker.

The Anonymous waka is #1025 from *Kokin Wakashū* and translated by Edward Seidensticker.

The scattered snapshots are small objects that I hope create a kind of autobiography. Although not artfully taken, I hope they amuse.

A number of these poems are "ghosts" of a sestina, quartina, pantoum, and glosa. Also, marriages of the cento and pantoum or villanelle.

The golden shovels make use of work by poets whose names appear in the subtitle. Richard Wright's is from his extraordinary final collection, *Haiku: The Last Poems of an American Icon* (New York: Arcade, 2012). The Japanese haiku were translated by Hiroaki Sato and can be found in *On Haiku* (New York: New Directions, 2018). Over the years I have benefited greatly from his friendship and permission to use his translations for my own purposes and I am very much in his debt.

"Found Lines for a Ghazal on Water" uses lines from "Clean Water Laws Are Neglected, at a Cost in Suffering," Charles Duhigg, *New York Times*, 9/13/09.

"Found Lines for a Ghazal on *Nearly 1,000 Birds*" uses lines from "Nearly 1,000 Birds Die After Striking Chicago Building" by Amanda Holpuch, *New York Times*, 10/8/23.

Regarding the erasures:

For "Erasing the *Ghost Forest*," the source text was Moises Velasquez-Manoff with Gabriella Demczuk photographs, "As Sea Levels Rise, So Do Ghost Forests," *New York Times*, 10/11/19.

For "Erasing *Honor*," the source text was "With Help, Afghan Survivor of 'Honor Killing' Inches Back" by Alissa J. Rubin, *New York Times*, 12/1/12.

For "Erasing *Love*," the source text was "Oarfish Offer a Chance to Study an Elusive Animal Long Thought a Monster" by Douglas Quenqua, *New York Times*, 11/2/13.

Regarding the poems in the *Likeness* section, I have used material from the following:

For "Survival: zombie bees": "Who's in Charge Inside Your Head?" by David P. Barash, *New York Times*, 10/6/12.

For "Unforgiving: snow leopard": "Saving More Than Just Snow Leopards" by Peter Zahler and George Schaller, *New York Times*, 2/1/14.

For "Virulent: Emerald Ash Borer": "The Slow Process of Countering the Emerald Ash Borer" by Carl Zimmer, *New York Times*, 8/27/15.

For "Lonesome Kimiko": "A Giant Tortoise's Death Gives Extinction a Face" by Carl Hulse, *New York Times*, 7/2/12.

For "The Moss Piglet": *Tardigrade: Wikipedia.*

For "Learning from a Murder": "Crows May Learn Lessons from Death" by Carl Zimmer, *New York Times*, 10/3/15.

Acknowledgments

First, my heartfelt thanks to the editors of my previous books at Kaya Press and Hanging Loose Press. In particular, dear Robert Hershon.

Acknowledgments for earlier poems appear in respective collections. These include numerous references to journals and books.

And now, my gratitude to those who accepted the poems for *The Ghost Forest, Likeness,* and *Toying* sections.

Alaska Quarterly Review
"Lonesome Kimiko"

American Poetry Review
"[Blossoming purple]"
"Climate-Change Driven Winds Across Nonnative Grasslands Leave Maui Vulnerable
   on August 10, 2023"
"The Ghost Forest"
"Seeing Someone Seeing"
"[Onion]"

BOMB
"Erasing the *Ghost Forest*"
"[Inside my body]—sections iii., iv."

Boston Review
"Erasing *Love*"

Court Green
"After Sonnet #12"

Floodgates
"A Riotous Disorder"
"Seeing Someone Seeing"

Iowa Review
"The Calculation of Nothing"

Kenyon Review
"The Earth's Day"
"On *Viscera*"
"Seeing to Etiquette"

The New Yorker
"On *Pleasing*"
"To be a daughter and to have a daughter"

Offing
"In Our Living Room"
"*Organized Decays*"

Phantom Limb Press chapbook
"Erasing *Honor*"

Plume
"[*Doll-E-Drink 'n' Wet Set's miniature evenflo*]"
"[*Mouse Trap*]"
"[*Tiddlywinks*]"

poem-a-day (Academy of American Poets)
"Ode to 'When lilacs last in the dooryard bloom'd' "
"[The whale already]"

Poetry
"Against Opulence"
"Anaphora Using the Wilfred Owen Line 'If you could hear, at every jolt' "
"Contrapuntal Opening with a Line from Millay"
"Convergence, an *ars poetica*"
"*if* is a conjunction"
"[Inside my body]—section ii."
"Not Nothing Again"
"A Revelation with Two Lines from Yeats"
"Villanelle with a Line Borrowed from Bishop"

Poet's Country
"Learning from a Murder"
"The Moss Piglet"

Prairie Schooner
"[Follow wherever]"
"The Toxicologist at Home"
"[The women first]"

The Progressive
"Found Lines for a Ghazal on Water"

A Public Space
"[I am paying]"

Quarterly West
"[a wind blows in]"

Spellbound Anthology (Everyman Books)
"ABRACADABRA"

Tribute to Walt Whitman chapbook (Brooklyn Public Library)
"Ode to 'When lilacs last in the dooryard bloom'd' "

(Write it!)—Odes to Lines chapbook (Wells College Press)
"Ode to 'Not for these / the paper nautilus / constructs her thin glass shell.' "
"Ode to 'When lilacs last in the dooryard bloom'd' "

Writing the Land Anthology
"Ode to the Mud in Corona Park"

Zone3
"Survival: zombie bees"
"Unforgiving: snow leopard"

Maybe she did pocket a few white stones for the moonlight. I know I hid pebbles to scatter, to find my way home. To a door. To a reflection.

I know I thought I had no one to guide me—but I did. I see now that I did. Some were in the next room. Some across a kitchen table.

I know I would not have reached this juncture without years of Jill Bialosky's thoughtful and keen suggestions. Very occasionally she encouraged me to trim or write more. I am grateful that she led me to see the whole in various ways, to offset or fold in. (And, in turn, I have used such magic with my students.) And I am full of thanks to Jan Heller Levi who spent hours rereading my collections to advise on this one. As in the past, there are poets who took time from their writing to comment on mine—Lee Briccetti, Nicole Cooley, Lynn Emanuel, Anne Marie Macari, Abby Wender. Thank you. And younger writers who are supportive in a great many ways—Nicole Sealey, Rajiv Mohabir, and Rigoberto González. Thank you. And, of course, Harold Schechter, my "research assistant" and beloved, has shared and suggested in ways conscious and dreamlike. Thank you! To his sweet daughters Elizabeth and Laura, thank you! And there are others who I've thanked in previous collections—thank you again!

My deepest thanks to the Poetry Foundation for the honor of the Ruth Lilly Lifetime Achievement Prize. It is humbling to receive such affirmation in one's later years.

I know, too, how fortunate I am to have these three charming women in my life—Reiko, Miyako, and Tomie. And I miss those to whom I dedicated my first book—Mother and Father. They gave me light, noise, scent, feelings. And words.

An air pocket of ayres.

A tansu of renga.

Index of Titles

Index of First Lines